RAISING

UNICORNS

INCLUDES THE RAINBOW-FILLED
PRINCIPLES OF UNICORNOMICS!

YOUR STEP-BY-STEP GUIDE TO
STARTING AND RUNNING A SUCCESSFUL—
AND *MAGICAL*—UNICORN FARM

JESSICA S. MARQUIS   *Illustrated by Kevin Hedgpeth*

AVON, MASSACHUSETTS

Published by
Adams Media, a division of F+W Media, Inc.
57 Littlefield Street, Avon, MA 02322. U.S.A.
www.adamsmedia.com

ISBN 10: 1-4405-2590-0
ISBN 13: 978-1-4405-2590-2
eISBN 10: 1-4405-2704-0
eISBN 13: 978-1-4405-2704-3

Printed in the United States of America.

10   9   8   7   6   5   4   3   2   1

Library of Congress Cataloging-in-Publication Data
is available from the publisher.

Illustrations © 2011 by F+W Media, Inc.

*This book is available at quantity discounts for bulk purchases.
For information, please call 1-800-289-0963.*

To Farmer McCready and Farmer McGlitter, pioneers, innovators, and icons in the fantastic world of unicorn farming.

CONTENTS

INTRODUCTION

Welcome to the whimsical and very lucrative world of unicorn farming! This is an industry like no other with potential limited only by your imagination.

By selecting this book, you are demonstrating four things:

1. You are an intelligent businessperson.
2. You know what you want.
3. You are ready to embrace the challenge and reap the rewards.
4. You are clever, charming, and jam-packed with moxie.

Sound like you? Then you have come to the right place.

As a future unicorn farmer, you will experience the wide and unique array of opportunities, challenges, and joys of caring for these majestic creatures. Use this guide to inform your decisions so you can grow as an educated proprietor—and achieve your most magical dreams.

This guide is divided into four sections to assist you in your business planning, execution, and the collection of feedback. Note that, in this case, execution means the carrying out of your plan, not the murder of your unicorns. That is almost entirely contrary to the purpose of this guide.

In the pages that follow, you will be led through the critical steps to fashion and unleash your unique unicorn-farm legacy on the unsuspecting populace, your future customers. In Part 1: Strategy, you will read about exploring and establishing a strategy to mark your territory in this hyper-fertile market. Part 2: Caring for Your Unicorns will teach you about this noble and profit-propagating type of livestock. In Part 3: Implementation, you will learn the strategies needed to develop the unicorn farm of your dreams and mercilessly crush your competition. Lastly, Part 4: Diagnosing Success will evaluate and maximize your earning potential.

And now onto your rainbow-filled adventure into the world of raising unicorns, using the enchanted pragmatic principles of Unicornomics!

WHICH TYPE OF UNICORN FARMER ARE YOU?

1. *You have just received a fully functional unicorn farm as a gift. What is your first action?*

   A. Assess the business and analyze the financial results. Identify and capitalize on its core competencies.
   B. Throw a party with the unicorns!
   C. Knock it down and move the unicorns into temporary housing. I have a better idea.
   D. Forget about it for a few months.

2. *You first became interested in unicorn farming when:*

   A. I read about the limitless unicorn business opportunities in *Forbes*.
   B. I saw a picture of a unicorn happily munching on rainbow hay and wondered, "How can I get one of those?"
   C. I was born.
   D. I got kicked out of my parents' basement and was told to get a job.

3. Your favorite aspect of the unicorn is:

A. Whatever sells best—or creates the items that sell best.
(B.) Its purity. And its whimsy. And its all-around awesomeness.
C. The boundless potential of its magic.
D. It's not real, so it can't hurt me.

4. Your prize unicorn is sick. What is your most urgent concern?

A. Will it be healthy enough to win at the races this Saturday?
(B.) How much chicken soup and cuddling is too much?
C. That is the unicorn doctor's job. I need to work on bigger farm stuff.
D. Avoiding serious issues like this.

5. Your unicorn farm has not made a profit in seven years. What is your plan?

A. Analyze my revenue trends and gross-profit margins. Focus on the lines of business that drive revenue and grow my top line. Meanwhile, control costs by scaling back on hiring, streamlining operations, and reducing discretionary spending.
(B.) It'll all work out. Unicorns are involved.
C. I am more focused on creating history than on turning a profit. (My financial advisor is handling communications with the stakeholders.)
D. Sell it to the highest bidder, regardless of his or her reputation.

6. One phrase that describes me as a unicorn farmer is:

A. "Success-seeking capitalist."
B. "Laid back but fabulous."
C. "Focused yet imaginative."
D. "Not into it."

7. The last thing on my unicorns' schedule each night is:

A. A strenuous workout to ensure health and fitness for ultimate productivity.
B. Frolicking together and eating ice cream.
C. The handlers take care of the schedule details. I just want to make sure we're on track for the farm to be functioning in outer space in three years.
D. Fending for themselves.

Mostly A's: Unicorn Tycoon. You come bearing budgets, profit projections, and strategic plans for expansion and market dominance. The unicorns know their place as products and/or producers, and they bow in reverence to your cash-generating expertise.

Mostly B's: Que Sera, Sera. You take business and life as it comes and cheerfully glide among the candy-coated clouds in a blissful state of unconditional acceptance. You get to hang out with unicorns! Why *wouldn't* you be happy all the time?

Mostly C's: Visionary. You like to build it from hoof to horn, redefining and reimagining unicorn farming. A big-picture thinker, you surround yourself with a team of experts to address the details. You have a dream leading the way, and that dream happens to have unicorns in it. But it is not girly.

Mostly D's: You should not be a unicorn farmer.

PART 1

STRATEGY

CHAPTER 1

PLANNING YOUR FARM

Before it is born into existence, every business destined for wild success requires a plan.

Unicorn farming is no exception.

In fact, it may require *more* forethought than most businesses, as there is a wealth of misinformation, with results ranging from minor nuisances to grave consequences.

A simple example can illustrate this point. It is a common belief that the unicorn is a docile creature. This misconception originates from the fact that they are typically observed while engaged in routine: They drink from a shimmering stream, chase the fluttering butterflies, then rest in a field of fresh green grass. However, if a unicorn's routine is disrupted, he can exhibit his disorientation by thrashing his hoofs and skewering with his horn.

Didn't know that? Good thing you do now, right? Well then, this book has already paid for itself.

This chapter will inform you about other particularly essential unicorn points (no horn pun intended) so you can become an educated unicorn farmer. In so doing, it will walk you through the development of your business strategy, from conception to Part 3: Implementation.

DO I WANT A UNICORN FARM?

Before you sign the lease for this farm, it is crucial that you have some familiarity with the substance with which you are filling it. There are many types of farms that exist, and all have their benefits and liabilities. The "Different Types of Farms" table offers a comparison of three popular types of farms: Crops (FIG. 1.a.), Unicorns (FIG. 1.b.), and Elk (FIG. 1.c.).

FIGURE 1.a. *Crops.*

FIGURE 1.b. *Unicorns.*

FIGURE 1.c. *Elk.*

DIFFERENT TYPES OF FARMS			
TRAITS	CROPS	UNICORNS	ELK
What does my farm produce?	Vegetables, fruits, trees, cotton, tobacco	Unicorns, dreams, happiness	Elk
Who are my customers?	Farmers' market junkies, organic boutiques, and supermarkets	Anyone who believes	N/A
What are the benefits?	Using what you produce; being able to provide others with consumable goods	Unicorn rides; ring-tossing games; wishes come true	Whenever someone asks if anybody has an elk, you can say, "I do"
What are the liabilities?	Lack of income due to crop disease; potential for crops to prove harmful to consumers; Children of the Corn sometimes wreak havoc on unsuspecting villagers	Vomit stains that are very difficult to get out of clothing; unicorns can exhibit unexpected magical powers at inopportune times	You run an elk farm

Now that you have the information necessary to make an informed decision, you can elect to continue with this guide, or find one on another farming topic of your liking.

Still reading? Good. Glad to see you made the right choice.

WHAT DO I WANT TO DO WITH MY UNICORN FARM?

One of the unique benefits of a unicorn farm is its versatility. When someone announces that he or she is a unicorn farmer, most people don't know what that means.

There are many options as to how to utilize your unicorn farm. Below is a list of the most popular by percentage. This table does not speak to revenue; that will be covered in Chapter 4: Developing Your Business Plan.

UNICORN BUSINESS POPULARITY BY PERCENTAGE	
UNICORN INDUSTRY	PERCENTAGE
Petting farm	22.7%
Breeding, raising, and grooming for sale	19.3%
Harvesting	15.6%
Unicorn refuge	15.3%
Harnessing magical powers for good	10.5%
Harnessing magical powers for evil	6.2%
Just for the heck of it	5.9%
Other	4.5%

ℰ *TESTIMONIAL* ℒ

STEPHANIE: REALTOR TURNED IMAGINATOR

Stephanie's father had always told her there was no job field more lucrative than real estate. She achieved high success as an agent, but frequently found herself wondering, "Where's the magic?" It wasn't until her eleventh year in the business that she came across a client looking for 75 acres of land. When she asked him his purpose for so much acreage, he responded with two words that changed her life forever: unicorn farming. Stephanie quit her job the next day and never looked back. She tells the audiences who attend her sought-after *Unicorn Farming for Novices* seminar series (based on her bestselling book and gold-record audiobook), "Forget real estate — the future is in unicorns!"

Some aspiring unicorn farmers mistakenly believe that there is a market for unicorn meat. Unfortunately for them, it is often after they have slaughtered a sizeable portion of their cattle that they discover that a unicorn carcass is of no use to anyone. Remember this rule of thumb:

Unicorn living: magic it's giving.
Unicorn expired: magic retired.

Nevertheless, as some experimental unicorn farmers have come to discover, anything harvested from a unicorn *while she is still alive* is unfathomably delicious. Both the horn and the meat have become rare delicacies to those who dare to acquire them. Yet, while this practice can lead to substantial profits for a radical farmer, it can also lead to you being blacklisted by all respectable unicorn proprietors and the unicorns themselves. Best bet: Let your livestock keep their shoulders and horn tips intact, which are the two tastiest parts of the unicorn.

ℰ CASE STUDY ℛ

HUNGRY PERRY

Perry entered the world of unicorn farming with the notion that the end goal was meat on the table. He enjoyed a balanced meal, however, so he also planted a variety of crops on his other plots of land. The corn grew and the tomatoes ripened, and Perry and his family planned a large celebration for the first harvest. The first 100 of the 2,000 guests had already arrived when Perry began the unicorn roast. Within seconds, a vacuum of magic caused all the crops to transform into rotting detritus, and Perry was left with nothing more than meat of a lower quality than hot dogs. The guests left in various states of melancholy, and the farm closed the next day.

TAKE IT WITH YOU!

1. There is considerable misinformation out there regarding unicorns that could result in death—yours or theirs.
2. Select the type of farm that best fits you. Try to avoid elk farming if you care about your image.
3. How you utilize your farm is important to your bottom line.
4. It is a best practice in unicorn farming to avoid killing your unicorns.

READER'S NOTES:

_____

_____

_____

_____

_____

_____

_____

_____

_____

_____

_____

_____

_____

CHAPTER 2

....

THE MAGIC OF RESEARCH

Anyone can buy a unicorn. Taking custody of some old unicorn isn't all that impressive if you don't know what it is you are purchasing. And there can be consequences to going into this type of ownership blindly. Indeed, making the wrong decision can be worse than remaining at a place of indecision!

This chapter will lead you on the captivating quest of gathering information to make an informed decision. Unleash the wonder!

WHAT TYPES OF UNICORNS EXIST?

This is a question that will help to further narrow down your purpose. Unbeknownst to medieval artists and porcelain-figure manufacturers, there is more than one breed of unicorn. Knowledge of each type and its characteristics will guide you as you work toward your defined business goals.

BREEDS OF UNICORNS

BREED NAME	APPEARANCE	LIFE EXPECTANCY	BEST FOR...
Purebred (Fig. 2.a.)	White as the driven snow; blue or lavender eyes; single horn on center of forehead; glitter in mane	Until it is caught by a man and loses its magic	Their kind nature allows for petting farm participation; little girls' drawings
Twinkletoe (Fig. 2.b.)	Glitter on body, mane, horn, and hoofs; green eyes; single horn on center of forehead	Until it is caught by a man and loses its magic	Raising and grooming for sale; glitter for little girls' art projects
Karmic (Fig. 2.c.)	Ivory body; red eyes; horn divides in two at tip	Until it is caught by a man and loses its magic	Irritable dis-position and anger-generated momentum, which can be captured as excellent sources of alternative energy
Gigglerump (Fig. 2.d.)	Stockier than Pure-bred; asymmetrical face with short horn on browline over right eye; dishwater-blond, scraggly mane	Unknown (no one has cared enough to track it)	Harvesting; slapstick comedy shows
Horse with Horn (Fig. 2.e.)	Brown, gray, white, or black; cardboard cone on elastic strap placed on forehead	20–30 years	Kids' parties when you can't afford a real unicorn and don't care about maintaining the illusion

FIGURE 2.a. *Purebred.*

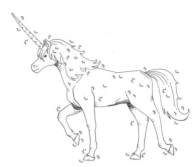

FIGURE 2.b. *Twinkletoe.*

FIGURE 2.c. *Karmic.*

FIGURE 2.d. *Gigglerump.*

FIGURE 2.e. *Horse with Horn.*

It is important to note that three of the breeds lose their magic when they realize they have been caught by a man. Not *the* man—unicorns shy away from statements of social activism— but *any* anatomically equipped man.

Therefore, if you are bringing them in from the wild, have a woman catch your unicorns. This will be addressed further in Part 3: Implementation. Nonetheless, this point needs to be clarified, as it has provided a tragic dead end to many male unicorn farmers.

To breed unicorns, the most ideal pairing is two Purebreds simply because of the sheer beauty. This is not to imply that a unicorn farmer should *observe* the actual act, but to do so is not as emotionally scarring as witnessing the mating ritual of the Gigglerump.

To answer the most frequently asked question of unicorns, yes, all breeds can mate successfully . . . depending on one's definition of success.

FANCY FUN FACT

Within the unicorn population, there are males, females, and switchers. The switchers can choose from moment to moment which sex they wish to be. However, if a switcher gets pregnant, she will stay female during the entire duration of the pregnancy. Because they dread the unpredictable surges of hormones that can disrupt routine, most prefer to stay male during mating season.

On average, it takes six attempts to result in a unicorn baby, which is called an "acorn" (FIG. 2.f.) since it is born without a horn. (Unicorn mothers are grateful for this.)

FIGURE 2.f. *An acorn.*

The acorn can choose to grow a horn at six months of age; if it chooses to do so, it needs to earn the horn. This is accomplished through acts of courage, altruistic deeds, and the successful befriending of a samurai.

If the acorn chooses not to earn its horn, it is resigned to the status of a "pretty pony." The development-arrested pony can still lead a fairly fulfilling life of eating, sleeping, and prancing, but it falls asleep each night with the nagging existential guilt of "What if?" Plus, little girls gravitate toward these ponies the quickest, and are not kind with their brushes and half-nelson hugs.

In regard to reproduction, the gestation period is the shortest for the Karmic: three days. This is in comparison with the longest of gestation periods: thirty-one months for the Purebred.

If you do the math, this means that you can have a farm full of angry unicorns exponentially more quickly than establishing a quiet petting zoo. This is one of the causes of the sudden upsurge in reports of unicorn stampeding. Unfortunately, at the time of this book's printing, Unicorn Anti-Stampede Initiatives have only been instated in Wyoming and the eastern half of Rhode Island.

ATTENDING A UNICORN SHOW

Selecting your livestock requires a wide variety of choices, close attention to detail, and a cash-invoking vision. The first require-ment can be found at a unicorn show. The last two are your responsibility, but if you attend snake-oil demonstrations enough you might find a sure-fire method to help you with at least one of them.

Similar to a state fair but with fewer fried-food oddities, a unicorn show brings together numerous buyers and suppliers of unicorns and related accou-trements. They tend to occur in public places that are easily acces-sible, and parking is regulated by the Unicorn Show Association (USA) (FIG. 2.g.) at $10 per day. This was decided following a USA settlement when a well-respected farmer was denied entrance upon attempting to use a jar full of chil-dren's dreams (FIG. 2.h.) to pay for parking.

FIGURE 2.g. *The logo of the Unicorn Show Association (USA).*

USA has been involved in establishing and maintaining high-quality unicorn shows for more than forty years. However, as professional organizations have become more plentiful and purveyors of fine unicorns and paraphernalia have gone rogue, the influence of USA at unicorn shows has waned. Its remaining jurisdiction is parking regulation, although it has some say in concession stand offerings.

FIGURE 2.h. *The infamous jar of children's dreams.*

As a visitor to a unicorn show, it is wise to carry your wallet in a fanny pack. This will protect your money from being taken by trolls that sometimes attach themselves to undersides of unicorns (FIG. 2.i.).

FIGURE 2.i. *A troll attached to the underside of a unicorn.*

WARNING: Politely decline any invitations to unicorn shows run out of a basement of an abandoned warehouse. They rarely have anything other than three-legged Gigglerumps.

Most sellers are aware of this parasitic form of transportation and are adept at identifying and extricating the trolls; however, newer or less-observant sellers may miss them, and this potentially leads to an infestation of tiny ugly pickpockets. This is the only time that wearing a fanny pack is advisable, and the pack should be immediately removed upon exiting the show.

FANCY FUN FACT

Pegacorns have grown in both popularity and population since their worldwide introduction during the 1980s. While they had existed for eons prior, few unicorn farmers wished to voluntarily care for both the temperamental nature of the Pegasus and the attention-craving disposition of the unicorn. However, when those farmers had the opportunity to soar high and fast into the clouds on the Pegacorn, they had an abrupt change of opinion. Since that time, numerous companies have emerged specializing in fortifying the walls, ceilings, and security systems for unicorn farms that raise these strong, moody, and escape-prone Pegacorns.

Most unicorn shows have one entry fee that grants anyone general admission to peruse the vendors and displays, but there is a growing demand for exclusive engagements for the discerning unicorn farmer. The first of these upscale shows occurred in Dubai, and was reported to debut a pegasus-unicorn hybrid named the Pegacorn. Since then, reports of such engagements have come from Vancouver, Montevideo, Tel Aviv, and Reykjavík. As of the writing of this guide, USA was not regulating parking for these shows.

For a first-time visitor to any show, the key is to arrive early and visit every stall. Before examining any unicorns, consult Chapter 8, which further explains the procurement of unicorns. Prepare a list of questions that can help you in assessing attractiveness, responsiveness, and durability. Here are some suggested questions for you to ask the seller:

- How did you acquire this unicorn?
- What is his or her best quality?
- How much can he or she lift?
- How much do you think I can lift?
- How does he or she get along with others (e.g., unicorns, children, clumsy farmhands)?
- What is his or her greatest weakness?
- If he or she could have dinner with anyone living or dead, what would the main course be?
- Has he or she been exposed to any radioactive compounds? If so, did he or she develop superpowers or health problems?
- What is your return policy?
- What is your free trial policy?

Do not ask if the unicorn farts glitter. At the very least, it will result in a raised eyebrow and a higher asking price. Nevertheless, if your curiosity is sincere, couch the question in this way: "What is the color and coarseness of the glitter emitted by this unicorn's flatulence?"

ℰ CASE STUDY ℊ
OVERDRESSED AND UNDERPREPARED STEVE

Steve hadn't quite grasped the concept of unicorns when he agreed to buy his ailing father's unicorn farm. On the first morning of his new role as farmer and owner, he realized that he had not restocked supplies for the livestock. Though dressed for the part with a straw hat and overalls, his fashions were no match for the demands of the farm. His lack of research led to the gradual demise of the farm, as well as his father's reputation. Blacklisted by the USA, he could no longer park at unicorn shows, and he eventually sold the farm and its remaining livestock to an international venturer who was looking for a new business plan after conquering rock music and outer space.

UNICORNOMICS PRINCIPLE

As the buyer of a unicorn in a competitive market, always ask for better incentives. Like a second unicorn.

VISITING OTHER UNICORN FARMS

If you are looking for more opportunities to examine and potentially purchase unicorns, consider visiting other farms. You not only will be able to observe the unicorns in a more natural setting, but you'll also be able to gather information on the internal processes of a unicorn farm much easier when you can copy from someone else's farm.

When you first enter the unicorn farm, identify yourself as a fellow farmer. If you wish to stay anonymous, be prepared to feel patronized—farm tours are typically designed for a less-savvy visitor.

What are you looking for on these visits? Input! So don't go around giving them advice. Keep your mouth shut and absorb their best and worst practices. Then try to forget the worst practices so you don't get them mixed up with the best practices.

WARNING: Do not trust a head unicorn farmer with a mustache.

FIGURE 2.j. *A head unicorn farmer with a mustache.*

After visiting with the livestock and touring the facilities, ask to meet with the head farmer. Titles of this individual may be any of the following: Director of Farming Practices, Farm Supervisor, or Unicorn Capo. The head farmer should be able to answer any questions you have regarding starting up your own farm. That is, unless he or she has a mustache.

Barring any mustachioed advisor, the tips you receive will be useful and should be recorded in some manner so you can implement them when you return to your property. Common questions asked of head unicorn farmers include:

- How many unicorns should I have to start my farm?
- What is the best way to get employees to work for wishes instead of money?
- How quickly can I take my business public?
- What is the cheapest but most effective bedding material?
- How can I increase revenue after selling off my top-racing unicorns to cover my gambling debt?
- Are unicorns cheaper if made in China?

If you decide to purchase a unicorn during your visit, be prepared with a competitive-pricing analysis. Farm visits are notorious for resulting in overpriced purchases due to visitors' perception of the status of the establishment, much like art museum gift shops. The following graph displays a comparison of sample unicorn costs by venue.

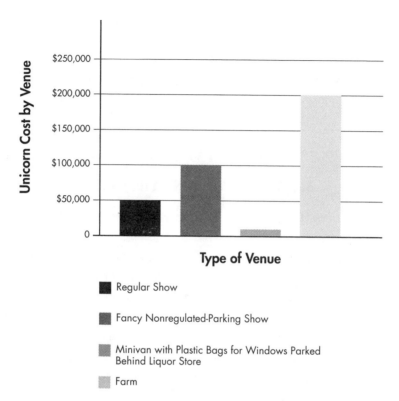

UNICORNOMICS PRINCIPLE

Never buy a unicorn that is more expensive than your farm.

When you have completed your visit to the unicorn farm, mail the head farmer a thank-you card immediately. This acts as a goodwill gesture to the rest of the unicorn-farming community, and it also keeps your handwriting skills from getting rusty.

ᘒ *TESTIMONIAL* ᘒ

MARVIN AND THE FANTASTIC CANDLES

Marvin spent the first half of his life without friends. He was rarely invited to sit with others at lunch, and the bus seats next to him went mostly unoccupied. It was a life-changing moment when, in college, he discovered that his roommate's mother was in the unicorn-wax candlemaking business. "I asked her if I could come over during winter break, and she thought it was to hang out with her son. I told her that I wanted to see the unicorns." As he watched her care for the ears of the wax-producers, he felt a connection to this type of business. He asked her how she found the unicorns—and what were the best parts of being a unicorn-wax candlestick maker? "She was surprised that I was so interested, since her son had always been embarrassed by her work. This visit inspired me to switch my major from nursing to business, graduate with honors, and open my own unicorn farm instead of attending commencements. I mean, no one was coming to them anyway," says Marvin.

TAKE IT WITH YOU!

1. All unicorns are not created the same, although they appreciate the sentiment of equality.

2. There are four main breeds of unicorns: Purebred, Twinkletoe, Karmic, and Gigglerump. A horse with a horn is not actually a unicorn.

3. Unicorns lose their magic if a man catches them, so have women do the work there.

4. Breeding unicorns can be beautiful or traumatizing, depending on the pairing, and will result in an acorn—a baby hornless unicorn, who can choose if having a horn is the life for it.

5. Unicorn shows and other unicorn farms are excellent venues for livestock purchases, but question lists and competitive-pricing analyses should be developed in advance.

6. Thank-you cards are appreciated throughout the unicorn farming industry.

READER'S NOTES:

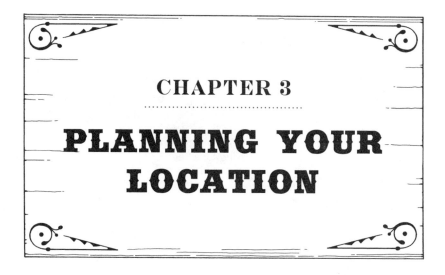

CHAPTER 3

PLANNING YOUR LOCATION

A philanthropic heiress once decided to use her inheritance to open a unicorn refuge. She spent nearly a year identifying the perfect lavender-scented, wheat-grass-adorned setting, then rescued nine unicorns from the local racetrack and set them free into the wonderland. What she hadn't taken into account was the frequency of lavender/wheat-grass allergies in racing unicorns, and they all immediately suffered extreme sinusitis.

This chapter will keep you from making a similar mistake.

When scouting a location for your future farm, consider the many phases of a unicorn's life (see the following chart).

All cycles but the last one take place on earth and indicate a need for positive and comfortable surroundings; even turning into an immortal deity on Mount Olympus is pretty great. Thus, unicorns desire pleasurable locations for their lifespan and beyond.

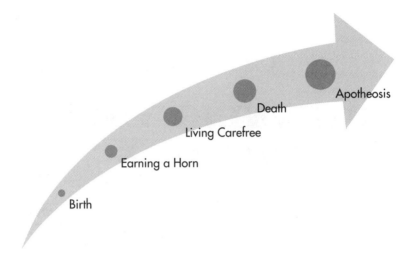

Apotheosis

Death

Living Carefree

Earning a Horn

Birth

BEST PLACES TO RAISE UNICORNS

Unicorns are self-sufficient and can make the best out of most situations. But don't let that fool you into thinking they are okay with second-rate accommodations. They can survive in all the biomes of the earth due to their innate ability to be awesome at just about anything, but unicorn-happiness levels are the highest in temperate deciduous forest, rainforest, and savanna biomes. The tundra is the least popular on the list, and unicorns dwelling in those areas are unabashedly passive-aggressive.

There has been some success with farms at sea, as long as a treaty has been established with the local narwhals. Unicorns that have been raised in these marine environments have medaled in swimming for the past four consecutive Mythical Olympic Games.

Other factors to consider when choosing locations to raise unicorns:

- Close proximity to a farmers' market with fresh, organic produce (FIG. 3.a.)
- Sunshine, interrupted by brief rainstorms followed by brilliant rainbows (i.e., Hawaii)
- Nearby responsible individuals who can unicornsit when you just need a night away from the farm

FIGURE 3.a. *An effective way to find a Farmers' Market.*

✃ *CASE STUDY* ✃
KEITH'S BRAZILIAN CAPER

It's unusual for a unicorn farmer to lose all his livestock within the first month, but Keith managed to do so. Upon winning a lottery of $2 million, Keith purchased the first unicorn-oil plantation he could find and moved his entire family into it. After all, he had always heard that oil was a big moneymaker; *unicorn* oil, he reasoned, must be even more so. Unicorn sebaceous glands are easily stimulated by humidity and the sight of waterfalls, producing oil that enhances the natural shine of unicorn coats. The farm was nestled in the Brazilian rainforest near seven different waterfalls, inducing each unicorn to produce up to two barrels of oil a week. When Keith took over operations, he removed the electric fencing his cousin had installed, believing it to be cruel. Guided by the misinformed assumption that a unicorn can always find its way home, he did not worry when they all walked out and into the rainforest. None returned.

WORST PLACES TO RAISE UNICORNS

If a unicorn desires a pleasurable location to carry out his innumerable days, it would beg to reason that an overstimulating, negative environment would have an adverse effect on him.

This is exactly what farmers at the New York City Unicorn Emporium discovered when it opened on 8th Avenue and 57th Street. Within trotting distance from Central Park, the idea was to let the unicorns bathe in the fountains and graze on the grass by day, offer rides to children and photo ops to tourists, and then let the unicorns rest in the skyscraper headquarters at night.

However, the unicorns' sleep schedules were thrown off immediately by the all-night traffic. The police car sirens and flashing lights around Central Park were constant. This stimulation, coupled with their lack of sleep, caused the unicorns to grow paranoid of their surroundings. By the time the unicorns had adjusted to the city noise, they were so convinced that there was nothing but violence and dead bodies in Central Park that they were afraid to leave the building. The Emporium closed the following week.

Additional failed city locations for unicorn farms include Hong Kong; Yakutsk, Russia; and Gary, Indiana. Flashing lights, frigid temperatures, and an abundance of gray in sky and land did not blend well with the unicorns' expectations.

Other factors to avoid when choosing locations to raise unicorns:

- Close proximity to glue manufacturers
- Nosy neighbors prone to gossip and slapstick antics
- Earthquake fault lines

HOW TO OVERCOME THE CONDITIONS OF THE AFOREMENTIONED WORST PLACES

Of course, sometimes the money in your pocket speaks louder than any "Best Places" list could. When you know what you want but can't conjure up the cash, remember this saying:

Wishing and hoping are better than moping!

Now, this isn't to say that wishing and hoping will create any kind of change in your situation, and you still need to take action on finding and opening your farm. However, a wishful, hopeful person is a lot more fun to be around than a grouch.

If you have examined your resources and can only afford a location that falls into the "Worst Places" list, have an honest heart-to-heart with your livestock. They would prefer you to be honest with them from the start, since they will find out eventually anyway. Tell them you would prefer better for them, and you have plans to improve their living situation, but right now this is the best your budget can do.

This meeting is pivotal, because it introduces the contagious start-up mindset that has led many Silicon Valley entrepreneurs to band together and give an incubating project 80 hours a week without question. You will see similar results from your unicorns.

Don't be surprised if suddenly an effervescent sapphire pond appears in the desert, and don't ask questions. Unicorns will give generously and unexpectedly, but they always want to keep their donations anonymous.

If no magic shows up, have some decent-quality AstroTurf on hand and some reliable contractors on speed dial. The minimal needs for starting a unicorn farm are water, food, waste-removal services, sleeping quarters, and fine art. Some of these items can double for others; for example, some large modern-art installations can provide adequate sleeping quarters, and waste can be burned for heat while the unicorns rest.

With these five items in place, despite an undesirable location, you can announce to the world that, yes, you are a unicorn farmer!

UNICORNOMICS PRINCIPLE

You can't get blood from a turnip—but unicorns can.

✶ *TESTIMONIAL* ✶

ROGER AND THE REALLY COLD RESORT

Minnesota's Oak Island was known only for cold temperatures and great fishing until Roger and his first Twinkletoe unicorn arrived in 1987. He knew his unicorn would go undisturbed by the few dwellers of the island, and the tourists were not the type to bother themselves with the business of unicorns. However, the cold temperatures and the lake surrounding them were both problematic for a creature with a coat composed primarily of sparkles and that struggled with a paralyzing fear of water. "I had two choices: Sink the cost and let that cold lake win, or trick my unicorn into thinking we were on a tropical peninsula." Roger chose the latter, installing sunlight-emulating lamps, heaters, and palm trees, and erecting a long soil-covered dock that the unicorn never walked on but assumed went to land. Word of his success spread rapidly, and his livestock grew exponentially. "My advice to someone with a unicorn farm—resort dream: Make sure you're near great fishing—it will make everything easier to deal with."

TAKE IT WITH YOU!

1. The location of your unicorn farm has an indelible impact on the success of the farm, since unhappy and/or dead unicorns don't benefit anyone.
2. The best locations for raising unicorns feature comfort, sunshine, and healthy dietary options.
3. The worst locations for raising unicorns feature overstimulation and sadness.
4. You can make a bad location good with some grit and unicorn buy-in.

READER'S NOTES:

_____

_____

_____

_____

_____

_____

_____

_____

_____

_____

_____

_____

_____

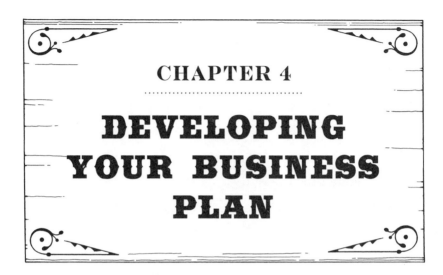

CHAPTER 4

DEVELOPING YOUR BUSINESS PLAN

At this point, you have formed the basics of your business plan: farming unicorns with a specific purpose in mind. You probably also have a good idea of which breed or breeds you want on that farm. Now the question arises of how to translate that plan into a giant magnet for the cash to make it all happen.

This chapter will address the questions that you have probably already been busy asking yourself. So stop wasting your time asking the questions, and let us ask them for you! (And then answer them for you!)

HOW DO I FUND MY UNICORN FARM?

Your purpose will help you to decide if this is a for-profit or nonprofit business, which determines potential funding sources.

If you are bringing unicorns to a local nursing home for pet therapy, you can establish a nonprofit organization with a touchy-feely human-interest title such as "The Healing Horn" (FIG. 4.a.). This enables you to apply for grants and do other things that not-for-profit groups do. Synergy!

FIGURE 4.a. *A senior citizen experiencing the magic of unicorn-petting therapy.*

✒ *TESTIMONIAL* ✒

CARLOS THE KARMIC KID

"I know a thing or two about unicorns, having been raised by two Karmics and their quirky neighbor the Gigglerump," Carlos says with pride. It was this deep connection forged during his childhood that led him as an adult to pursue his dream of creating a refuge for the creatures he loved so dearly. Having collected donations at sci-fi conventions, art festivals, and through his own creation, a Trot-a-Thon, Carlos immediately invested the money in a burgeoning stock market. By the end of the month, he had enough money to buy a small country, so that is what he did. He named it Unicornivia, removed evidence of it from all modern maps, and has used it as a private rehab-resort facility and, of course, a unicorn refuge. With fondness, he looks outside the giant bay window in the group therapy massage-and-manicure room to the alfalfa fields below. "I want the unicorns to feel as safe as they made me feel as a child."

But if you *really* want to make the big bucks, get ready to do some schmoozing with your well-dressed acquaintances and local monocle-bearing business honchos!

Here are some preferred ways to raise capital to make your foray into the unicorn business:

- Private investors
- Second mortgage
- Selling off all the stuff from your last major obsessive endeavor
- Booth at the local renaissance festival selling unicorn-related junk
- Borrowing from whimsical, flighty friends who won't question your reasoning

It may appear challenging to convince a private investor to hand over a check to buy a unicorn, especially if said investor is unconvinced of the creature's existence. This is why a compelling presentation must be prepared and on hand at any given opportunity.

In assembling this presentation, remember that *you* are in control. Concentrate on the fact that your audience wants to make money as much as you do. Believe that the power of the unicorn can make anything happen. Clap your hands if it makes you feel better.

Overheads, poster-board displays, and multiple-page handouts are traditional tools for these types of presentations. But what if you aren't in an office? What if a stranger stops you on the street one day as you are about to walk into your favorite gourmet sandwich shop, and he says to you, "I really want to make a ton of cash but don't know where to find a good investment. Do you have one?"

Well, do you?

This is why you *must* have an elevator speech ready at any moment. This is a thirty-second, irresistible pitch that captures the excitement of your business and incites an emotional response in your audience that causes them to shout out, "Here's my credit card with a $50,000 limit! Keep it! I won't report it missing!"

For the audience member who is less emotional and more data driven, be ready with some persuasive statistics. Most people know that 83 percent of statistics are made up on the spot, but only 17 percent realize this before they write the check.

WISDOM FROM A RETIRED UNICORN FARMER

If investors are angry after they write you a check because of your deliberate deception, be ready with a good lawyer. Don't use any more statistics to help you . . . unless they sound *really* convincing.

YOUR UNICORN FARM DREAM TEAM

Your dream of a unicorn farm may feature you as producer, director, actor, and gaffer, but the truth is that you will need a full cast and crew to make your farm run smoothly, safely, and for more than a week. So which star players should you hire first?

Obviously, you will need a doctor. An alchemist that specializes in unicornological sciences is preferred, although really any open-minded veterinarian will do.

When your unicorns arrive, they will need to be examined immediately before mixing with the others. Therefore the doctor should be there on day one. You can get around the high cost of employing a full-time doctor by making your arrangement contractual. This option has the added benefit of making readily available a contract that can be dramatically torn in two if and when you wish to stress a point to an underperforming doctor.

Stable hands and groomers are the next team members that the unicorn meets after the doctor. These individuals should be familiar with unicorn handling including diet, behavior, affect, and proper hygiene (for the unicorn and for themselves). You can often find excellent stable hands and groomers already working with horses, and all they need is some supplemental training on the subtle nuances that distinguish the horse from the unicorn. The individuals who are not as excellent can also be trained, but they should stay working with only the slow-but-kind-of-loveable-in-a-pathetic-way Gigglerumps.

Preferably, all of these employees will be virgins, as unicorns are more comfortable approaching and being approached by another pure creature. If you have hired virgins and then later find your unicorns behaving differently toward these employees, you then have some good fodder for gossip and/or blackmail.

This segues into a new employment concept that is gaining popularity in the unicorn-farming field: the On-Call Virgin (OCV) (FIG. 4.b.). These valuable employees are especially

FIGURE 4.b. *Business card of a successful OCV.*

effective with the Karmics, which frequently end up out of control. OCVs are called in to calm the Karmics and lead them toward a path of conformity to the farm rules. New farm insurance plans are currently under development specifically for the OCV position, addressing the liability that comes with approaching freaked-out, red-eyed unicorns.

Lastly, related to the previous section on angry investors, have a team of lawyers handy at all times. This not only protects you but also makes your business seem more legitimate. This way, when someone asks you a question for which you don't have an answer, you can reply, "Let me check with our lawyers, and I'll get back to you."

Presto: immediate credibility!

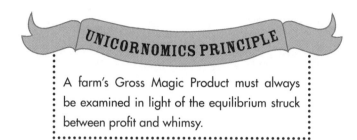

UNICORNOMICS PRINCIPLE

A farm's Gross Magic Product must always be examined in light of the equilibrium struck between profit and whimsy.

HOW DO I MAKE THE MOST MONEY?

Money flows easily with novelty, but there are ways to increase the flow and extend the novelty beyond the passing-fancy point. This has been accomplished with such items as platform boots, chocolate, and indoor plumbing. Domesticated skunks, on the other hand, have not fared as well.

The key is to make the product relevant to more than a niche market. In other words, don't cut off the possibilities at merely owning one Gigglerump, and don't settle for a marketing plan consisting solely of a dog-eared poster-board with "Come pet the unicorn!" scrawled in black marker.

You are opening a unicorn farm! That is the *impetus* to dream big!

Your farm can be the product, much like Disneyland. Advertise how unique and amazing it is to visit your farm and see the unicorns. Create an environment as close to their natural habitat as possible, complete with puffy clouds and soothing forest sounds. If the farm doesn't scream "bliss-inducing wonderland," install some kind of old-timey carousel on the grounds to jazz the place up.

Of course, merchandising is a great way to reach the masses. T-shirts (FIG. 4.c.), toys, and lawn plaques bearing ironic slogans are quick moneymakers. Mass produce the junk that hits it big with your customers.

People also appreciate functionality. Consider a great-tasting jam that is not made from unicorns (remember: they taste horrible)

FIGURE 4.c. *A unicorn-themed T-shirt available in unicorn gift shops.*

but has some glitter in it. Not too much glitter, though; that descends into unmitigated novelty. Unmitigated novelty should be only found at gift stores or in mail-order catalogs at your grandparents' house.

FANCY FUN FACT

Researchers at an alternative fuel lab in Sacramento, California, recently discovered that some Twinkletoes possess the ability to convert human gas to electricity. Much opposition has arisen from the animal rights community regarding employing unicorns as energy converters. They also see ongoing exposure to these noxious fumes as cruel to animals.

HOW DO I WRITE A MISSION STATEMENT TO INSPIRE MYSELF TOWARD GREATNESS?

If you were to ask the average crop farmer what his farm's mission statement is, he may stop chewing his straw of hay long enough to spit on your shoe. That is what separates unicorn farms from other farms: classiness.

Unicorn farmers tend to chew red licorice instead of hay, and they prefer to use their time to develop mission statements. A mission statement says what you plan to do. Mission statements are full of empowering action words that augment your professional image, making you feel like the ambitious and accomplished entrepreneur you want people to think you are.

Here are some examples of good and bad mission statements.

GOOD VS. BAD MISSION STATEMENTS	
GOOD	BAD
The mission of Unicorn Bonanza is to energize the unicorn-hair market with high-quality products and competitive pricing.	We want to divide you from your money. Forcefully.
The mission of Unicorn Vendors United is to spread love one unicorn, one rainbow, and one wealthy owner at a time.	Our mission is to completely disregard your well-being.
Unicorncentrated Juices, LLC aims to be the number-one choice of all unicorn-approved juices.	We strive to become a communist entity separate from the United States of America.

As you can see, the good mission statements entice you to feel safe about opening your wallet. You may know very little about the business, but the fact that a mission statement exists and it sounds like it is an informed assertion convinces you that this is a worthwhile establishment.

MOST PROFITABLE UNICORN VENTURES

By this time, you, the future unicorn farmer extraordinaire, are likely saying, "This is all well and good, but how can I make the most money?"

This question shows that you have the right motivation. After all, how can you win big if you keep playing the penny slots? The saddest stories of unicorn farm failures come from business owners who never aimed high and settled for mediocrity. Sure, they may *say* they are satisfied with their lot in life, content that they set attainable goals that are met each year, allowing their unicorns and employees to take holidays and sick days off. But how thick are their annual reports? How many colors can they afford to print them in?

Exactly.

The most profitable unicorn ventures are visible in the pie chart that follows, showing their share in overall profits during the past ten years.

With few exceptions, these categories have remained stable in their market share for the past decade. Still, don't let this decide for you which category you wish to dominate. You can be the anomaly within a category! For example, if you know you have an eye for talent, you will make more than the guy who opens a theme park with untested rides and has to pay out all his earnings for lawsuits.

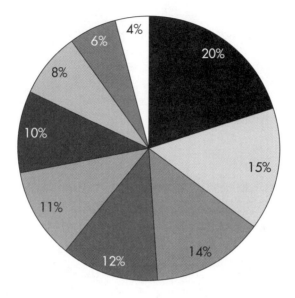

20% Tangible products (e.g., unicorn ivory products, hair extensions from unicorn hair, sparkling wine stomped by unicorns, etc.)

15% Personal services (e.g., transportation, acupuncture, service unicorns, etc.)

14% Petting zoos/Family fun farms (not part of parks)

12% Amusement parks (FIG. 4.d.)

11% Education centers

10% Commercial services (e.g., renewable energy, package, telegrams, etc.)

8% Racetracks

6% Entertainment (e.g., real magic shows, movie cameos, community theater, etc.)

4% Other

FIGURE 4.d. *A unicorn showcase at an amusement park.*

In addition to choosing the venture that best fits you, you will also need a sizeable chunk of perseverance. As with most entrepreneurial undertakings, unicorn businesses usually take five years to turn a profit. And sometimes that profit isn't money, especially if your clients are unicorns whose currency consists of rainbow slices. So hang in there—one day, you may be the one passing out the unicorn farm advice!

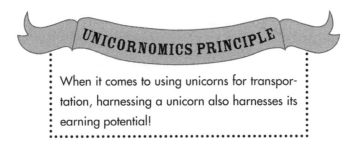

UNICORNOMICS PRINCIPLE

When it comes to using unicorns for transportation, harnessing a unicorn also harnesses its earning potential!

✒ *CASE STUDY* ✒

MARY'S MISGUIDED DREAM

Mary had dreamt of owning a unicorn-themed pizza restaurant and entertainment center for years. At age seven, she was drawing pictures of herself playing unicorn-themed pinball, and at fourteen she had written the first musical set for the animatronic stage performers. It was as she was working on her double-master's degree in Business and Robotic Engineering that she was introduced to the concept of unicorn racing. Abandoning her childhood dream, she poured all her money into purchasing a struggling racetrack and two Purebred-Karmic unicorns, bred to win and strike a peaceful fear into all competitors. The track was never able to stand alone financially, however; it folded—along with Mary's life savings. She still finds herself humming the opening number to the unicorn-robot singers' never-produced set, "Unicorns Love Pizza!"

TAKE IT WITH YOU!

1. Nonprofit businesses are nice and all, but for-profit businesses will make you rich and famous.
2. Always be armed with an awe-inspiring presentation and lightning-fast pitch on why people should give you their money.
3. Your farm will need a doctor, stable hands, groomers, lawyers, and at least one virgin. If you don't have the last one, look into OCV availability in your community.
4. To make money, figure out what your farm is all about and what about it is salesworthy. But always avoid unmitigated novelty.
5. Chew red licorice.
6. Customers love good mission statements.

READER'S NOTES:

_____

_____

_____

_____

_____

_____

_____

_____

_____

✎ PART 1 ✎
IN CONCLUSION

As this Strategy section ends, you now have a clearer picture of your business plan in this lucrative field. As dollar signs and unicorns waltz together in your mind's eye, it is time to start putting this plan into action.

Get out there and pull those fishnets full of cash into your pockets! And get some bigger pockets!

Go interview some promising candidates, always watching for a sign of wonder glistening in their eyes (they make the best salespeople).

Make an itinerary to visit several wooded wonderlands to round up the first of your cattle.

Visit a unicorn show with your wallet gripped tightly to subvert the stowaway trolls.

Get ready to work hard . . . with your imagination!

~ PART 2 ~

CARING FOR YOUR UNICORNS

CHAPTER 5

....

BECOMING FAMILIAR WITH THE ROUTINES OF UNICORNS

Any successful entrepreneur will tell you that your idea is only as good as its demonstration. You may have strategized up a storm during the last chapter, but high-impact unicorn farms don't jump out of strategy storms. They are birthed through the intercourse of wonder and action.

This chapter is about getting down to business, so if you want to daydream as you stare at cloud shapes, hang out in Chapter 1 some more.

The cash comes in when you create a desirable product or service. You can put a product or service out there without a plan, but it will not yield the same return as a plan with guidelines, objectives, goals, and business buzzwords.

What makes the balance within this type of industry particularly challenging to strike, though, is that no one can put parameters and box panels around anything related to a unicorn. Just when you think you have it down to a science, the unpredictable art of it emerges and head-butts your intentions and stock forecasting.

Building your plan and putting it into place is not as easy as it sounds. Be prepared to redefine some of your ideas as we approach Part 3: Implementation.

YOUR UNICORN: THE BASICS

Unicorns are more than just glitter and love. They have an anatomy full of wonder with which you as a farmer must be acquainted (FIG. 5.a.).

Unicorns are distant relatives of the oryx, narwhal, goat, and modern rhinoceros, and they are direct descendants of the hoplitomeryx, hexameryx, and ancient rhinoceros. However, the unicorn's horn ("alicorn") possesses a higher degree of magic than

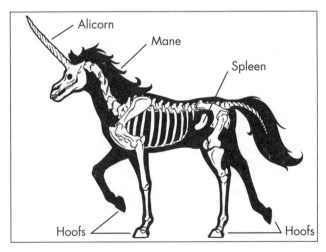

FIGURE 5.a. *A unicorn's anatomy.*

the horns of its family at approximately 3.6 deciliters, compared to an average of .03 microliters of magic found in the others.

In addition to the alicorn, there are three other parts of the unicorn anatomy that frequently emit magic: the mane, the hoofs, and the spleen. That totals four chances for wonder and amazement!

- **The alicorn** has a legendary reputation for repelling poison and removing toxins.
- **The mane,** when shaken vigorously, launches mutant dust mites into the air to create a distraction through allergic reactions in the enemy.
- **The hoofs** make chocolate chip cookies taste up to twenty-three times better.
- **The spleen** shoots rainbows out of various open orifices, which can serve as happiness transmitters or as lasers for annihilation, dependent upon breeding and training.

FANCY FUN FACT

With its demonstrated effectiveness at toxin elimination, the alicorn is a great detox treatment, unhealthy-relationship detector, and carpet-stain remover.

Other unicorn attributes of note are the saliva and mucus, both useful in the kitchen. Unicorn saliva is great for weight loss, as it causes food flavor to act inversely with calorie content, suppressing the flavor of high-calorie foods and increasing the flavor of healthier options. The mucus on the other hand, is filled with sparkles and is used to make rock candy.

✣ *TESTIMONIAL* ✣

KELLY THE COURAGEOUS

With severe allergies that required her to sleep wearing an oxygen mask, Kelly was unsure about buying her first unicorn. "I knew of the mutant dust mites contained in his mane, and I constantly feared him getting angry at me," she confesses. Still, she hated her job as a plastic surgeon and she wanted to follow the fulfilling and profitable career path of a unicorn farmer. So, with oxygen mask in place, she paid her $10 parking fee at the regional unicorn show and purchased her first two steeds. She found that after spending time with them each day, she began to develop immunity to her allergies. "The oxygen mask fell off one day as I was grooming Sugarlashes, and I could breathe clearer than ever before! I got more than I paid for when I started my unicorn farm — I got my health back. Plus, I'm making five times as much as I did doing rhinoplasty."

A popular activity throughout the ages has been to identify if a unicorn is really a unicorn or if he is a fraud. Impostors have included a goat with fused horns (FIG. 5.b.), an anorexic rhino (FIG. 5.c.), and a narwhal with prosthetic legs (FIG. 5.d.).

FIGURE 5.b. *A goat with fused horns.*

FIGURE 5.c. *An anorexic rhino.*

FIGURE 5.d. *A narwhal with prosthetic legs.*

Modern experts have found that you have two options to help with your unicorn detection:

- Examining the horn's chemical reaction to poison
- Using a virgin and seeing if the animal approaches

Keep in mind, the scientific method for the latter procedure is much more valid and reliable.

Unicorns tend to be monogamous, if they mate at all. While not a herding species, the unicorn is amiable enough to spend extended periods of time with other unicorns. A group of unicorns is informally referred to as a "polycorn posse," and a leader frequently emerges from within. The more formal title of "blessing" was created by greeting card companies in the same product-planning meeting as Boss's Day, and most unicorns refuse to acknowledge its use. Especially the males.

FANCY FUN FACT

Unicorns have a higher council to which they all ultimately report, the Assembly of the Unicorn Keepers, overseen by The Omnicorn. The Assembly is available to all unicorns to arbitrate difficult cases and hand down decrees, as well as to plan surprise parties for forgotten birthdays.

Unicorns are like humans in that they can be notably shrewd but simultaneously quite stupid. Another similarity is that, when frightened, they will defer to another that is more dominant, whether or not it is from the same gene pool. This, as logic would dictate, often leads to hilarious hijinks.

Unicorns can be superficial, and the cliques within a polycorn posse tend toward the snarky-detail fixation of celebrity-gossip reporters. As a result, in recent years, there has been a significant rise in fur highlights, horn augmentations, and teeth sharpening. While the first two treatments are for cosmetic purposes, the third is for combating the snarky comments.

The four breeds of unicorns are located throughout the world. Following is a map of where you will typically find each (FIG. 5.e.). Some countries take pride in their unicorn populations, such as Scotland, whose national animal is the Purebred. Other countries have downplayed or, in the case of France with their overwhelming number of Gigglerumps, denied the presence of their unicorns entirely.

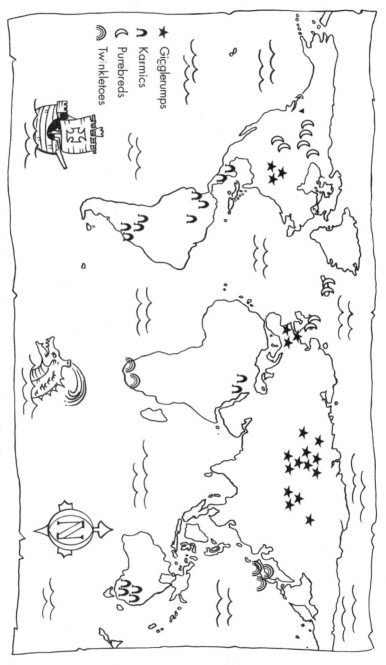

FIGURE 5.e. *A world map with the unicorn concentration within each country.*

Fun and freedom are integral to the unicorn lifestyle, and unicorns are not typically inclined toward working. Still, routine is natural to them.

A typical day in the life of a wild unicorn is scheduled in this way:

TYPICAL UNICORN SCHEDULE	
TIME	ACTIVITY
7:00 A.M.	Wake up to rays from the sun kissing my face
7:15 A.M.	Listen to the birds singing in the meadow
8:00 A.M.	Bathe in a glistening stream
8:30 A.M.	Run and play in the meadow
9:30 A.M.	Eat delicious grass
11:00 A.M.	Run and play in a nearby waterfall
1:00 P.M.	Nap beside aforementioned glistening stream
2:30 P.M.	Personal hygiene break
3:00 P.M.	Eat delicious berries
4:30 P.M.	Run and play in a nearby town at the foot of a supernatural mountain
6:00 P.M.	Eat a choice of delicious root vegetables or delicious table scraps from a guiltless, awe-struck child (based on availability)
7:30 P.M.	Cuddle/nuzzle time with polycorn posse
9:00 P.M.	Evening snack of ambrosia
10:30 P.M.	Be kissed goodnight by the moonbeams
10:45 P.M.	Sleep in a soft pile of some sort of natural bedding

While their lives are not the most interesting to observe, knowing their routines will assist in their detection, ambush, and capture.

WISDOM FROM A RETIRED UNICORN FARMER

If you don't have the time or money to tend to a full unicorn, consider ownership of a semicorn. This "unicorn-lite" option appears like a miniature unicorn in all features, but produces only one-third the magic. This results in lower feeding and re-energizing costs, yet still allows you to follow your dreams—at least, one-third of the way.

ℰ CASE STUDY ℛ

CHRIS AND THE CONFORMITY CONUNDRUM

Forever the impulsive type, Chris bucked routine whenever he encountered it. He was the cousin of a childless unicorn-oil tycoon, and inherited the entire operation upon his cousin's untimely death due to complications from cavities caused by chewing too much red licorice. It came as little surprise to his unicorn-farmer mentor, then, that his unicorns bucked Chris's leadership when he attempted to gain control of them. The mentor explained that Chris needed to establish and follow a routine to keep the unicorns happy and responsive. Chris filed away the advice in his mental trashcan and continued with his haphazard management. Unfortunately for Chris, the unicorns knew about at-will employment and quit without giving advanced notice. Chris finally accepted that he was not cut out to be a unicorn farmer and pursued his other dream of becoming an erratic rock star.

TAKE IT WITH YOU!

1. Although the entire unicorn is magical, the *most* magical parts are the alicorn, mane, hoof, and spleen.
2. There have been numerous unicorn impostors throughout the ages. Beware the faux enchantment of the anorexic rhino!
3. Unicorn relationships are complicated and full of ambivalence, much like those of humans.
4. Unicorns crave schedules and routines. Use this to your advantage.

READER'S NOTES:

_____

_____

_____

_____

_____

_____

_____

_____

_____

_____

_____

_____

_____

CHAPTER 6

THE EXPANSES AND LIMITS OF UNICORN MAGIC

Almost as legendary as the creatures themselves are the stories told of their magical abilities. From breath mints made entirely out of unicorn saliva to a submarine crew determined to find the lost city of Atlantis relying on a unicorn for its entire oxygen supply, countless unicorn professionals have found themselves in precarious situations due to this misinformation.

The following tables will help in dispelling some of the most notorious myths, perhaps revealing some helpful truths to extend the reaches of your business! Or at least preventing you from putting seven submarine crew members' lives at risk.

UNICORN MAGIC IN YOUR PERSONAL, DAY-TO-DAY LIFE

You may not yet think of unicorns as everyday fixtures, but their magic has many practical household and office-friendly applications. By familiarizing yourself with their functionality, you can increase your productivity. Synergy!

WHAT UNICORN MAGIC CAN AND CAN'T DO IN YOUR PERSONAL, DAY-TO-DAY LIFE	
WHAT UNICORN MAGIC CAN DO	**WHAT UNICORN MAGIC CAN'T DO**
Reclaim lost love	Justify stalking
Figure out your ex-coworker's unconventional filing system	Figure out your ex-spouse's unconventional thought system
Identify virgins	Identify difference between virgin olive oil and extra-virgin olive oil
Provide a wealth of resources while living	Make anything worthwhile when dead
Revitalize failing careers	Revitalize zombies
Breathe underwater	K.O. a manatee
Fold maps and flags correctly	Make anything more than a swan with a cloth napkin
Improve your crazy aunt's cooking skills	Improve your crazy aunt's conversational skills
Summon rainbows	Summon your cute neighbor whom you always see at the laundromat to go out with you
Accomplish the entire contents of a montage in real time	Secure pro-bono legal rights to "Eye of the Tiger"
Redirect awkward conversations	Keep said conversations from repeatedly venturing back to awkwardness
Answer all your unspoken questions in one answer	Take the place of real legal or medical advice

FANCY FUN FACT

Unicorns communicate with each other using a form of telepathy that can span up to 2,000 miles (3,218.7 kilometers) without interference. This system is also used when communicating with humans, but it occurs on a separate channel, much like a CB radio. As a result, humans will not hear a message in their heads to meet up at dawn for rainbow races—unless a unicorn forgot to switch the channel to Unicorns Only.

ℰ CASE STUDY ℒ

SYLVIA GETS REALLY SICK

Sylvia should have known better than to choose her unicorn's telepathic recommendations over her family physician, but she preferred the unicorn's suggested course of treatment. After two weeks of eating nothing but cotton candy and ice cream sprinkles, she concluded this wouldn't cure her rheumatoid arthritis and had to take a sabbatical from the farm to recover from severe pain and malnutrition.

UNICORN MAGIC IN ACHIEVING YOUR DREAMS, GOALS, AND FANTASIES

At the crossroad of fantasy and reality stands the unicorn, one foot in the present and one foot in the possible, and the other two feet are wherever they please. Why? Because it's a unicorn, and unicorns can do just about anything. Just about. How can a unicorn help you with your hopes and goals? Read on, golden dreamer.

WHAT UNICORN MAGIC CAN AND CAN'T DO FOR YOUR DREAMS, GOALS, AND FANTASIES	
WHAT UNICORN MAGIC CAN DO	WHAT UNICORN MAGIC CAN'T DO
Bend space-time continuum	Turn a wormhole into a rabbit-hole
Create new elements	Turn carbon dioxide into oxygen underwater
Fly	Help you get through airport security faster than anyone else
Control Daylight Savings Time	Convince everyone that Daylight Savings Time makes sense
Help you set New Year's resolutions	Implement New Year's resolutions that involve 5:00 A.M. gym attendance
Teletransportation	Reteletransportation to go back and turn off the light you left on in the den
Pull Santa's sleigh faster than any red-nosed reindeer	Discipline itself not to go into warp speed and/or outer space when pulling Santa's sleigh
Spin hay into platinum	Spin hay into plutonium
Improve study skills and information retention the night before an exam	Eat homework

WHAT UNICORN MAGIC CAN AND CAN'T DO FOR YOUR DREAMS, GOALS, AND FANTASIES (CONT'D)

WHAT UNICORN MAGIC CAN DO	WHAT UNICORN MAGIC CAN'T DO
Make it rain cupcakes	Arrange effective evacuation procedures in the case of a cupcake flood
Rewrite history	Make Victory Coffee taste good

ℰ *TESTIMONIAL* ℒ
CYRUS'S SECRET TO PUNCTUALITY

Cyrus had battled with tardiness all of his life. When he bought his first herd of unicorns, they were at first sympathetic to his quirks but eventually grew tired of his uncanny ability to be fifteen minutes late to everything. "I felt terrible," he recalls. "I began setting my clocks back twenty minutes to fix it, but it didn't help. I knew they wouldn't put up with it for too long, being the routine-huggers that they are." But to Cyrus's surprise, the unicorns took pity on him and used their time-bending powers to help him. Suddenly, Cyrus was on time — even early — to every commitment. "We all benefited from their charity. I may manage them in title, but they manage me even more." Cyrus is currently in talks with his unicorns regarding the possibility of marketing this power to college students and cable installers.

UNICORN MAGIC IN HEALING

For eons, unicorns and their horns have been the fallback plan for the medical community. "When all else fails, a unicorn won't," is the credo of the World Medical Association, the secret organization to which all medical professionals past and present have belonged. If you are wondering whether your condition can benefit from unicorn treatment, see the list that follows.

| WHAT UNICORN MAGIC CAN AND CAN'T DO IN HEALING ||
WHAT UNICORN MAGIC CAN DO	WHAT UNICORN MAGIC CAN'T DO
Regeneration of own limbs and ⅔ of alicorn	Cloning
Cure the common cold	Cure the uncommon cold
Heal physical wounds	Heal psychosomatic symptoms
Repel and neutralize poison	Get you out of going to your fifteen-year-old's high school performance of *Arsenic and Old Lace*
Counteract lactose intolerance and food allergies	Remove masking-tape residue from nosepiece of glasses
De-blight potatoes	Wipe out the collective memory of Olestra
Purify water from any water source	Keep faulty drinking fountains from spontaneously spraying you in the face
Prevent cholera with hugs	Nuzzle away smallpox
Inoculate you against salmonella using its saliva	Cure halitosis
Whittle a first-aid kit out of tree bark	Keep the bandages from giving you splinters
Transform freckles into wishes	Transform freckles into popularity

TAKE IT WITH YOU!

1. It is best to know what a unicorn can and can't do through its magic before taking a risk. This could save your life and/or your dignity.
2. Unicorn magic can be used in substantial issues, such as time travel, or small details, such as filing.
3. If a unicorn can't do something, don't insist that he or she can simply because a unicorn should be able to do anything.

READER'S NOTES:

_____

_____

_____

_____

_____

_____

_____

_____

_____

_____

_____

_____

_____

_____

_____
_____
_____
_____
_____
_____
_____
_____
_____
_____
_____
_____
_____
_____
_____
_____
_____
_____
_____
_____
_____
_____
_____
_____
_____

CHAPTER 7

UNICORN HAZARDS

"Raising unicorns isn't all rainbows and glitter."

—FARMER McSIMMONS

This quote has been uttered and muttered repeatedly throughout the past 250 years, since Farmer McSimmons first spoke it at the Council of Unicornologists meeting.

Besides their high-maintenance tendencies, unicorns are prone to numerous hazards. Not quite klutzes, but not the ballerinas of the equestrian persuasion portrayed in porcelain figurines and paint-by-numbers canvases, they keep their caretakers busy around the clock.

By entering into an owner/enchanting-chattel relationship, you assume responsibility for the chattel (assuming *you* are the owner). This means keeping them safe. This chapter will present the most common hazards, as well as proactive and reactive strategies.

COMMON HAZARDS AND PROPER RESPONSES

One, Two, Unicorn Stew
Made from a silly unicorn who
Got stuck in a fence
But was too dense
To use his magic as unicorns do.

This old-timey jump-rope limerick is a reminder of the unexpected nature of unicorn hazards. While their abilities are vast, their memories are short; their awareness is often compromised by a minor case of ADHD—as common in the females as in the males.

Unicorns are gullible, so a good unicorn farmer keeps a close eye on all interactions, especially those with strangers and bullies. Many a unicorn has wandered up to a beckoning van driver to find himself stashed in the trunk and on his way to a circus sideshow in a distant podunk town (FIG. 7.a).

This gullibility has also made them a popular target for pyramid schemes. These schemes spread like conjunctivitis at a poorly

FIGURE 7.a. *An ominous stranger using food to entice a unicorn toward an awaiting car trunk.*

managed day care, and soon all the unicorns are attempting to sell to one another.

However, not all hazards are related to gullibility. Besides the obvious hazards provided by the unicorn's enemies, which will be addressed in Chapter 9, a typical unicorn is also prone to health hazards, primarily the deviated septum, vertigo, and acid reflux.

The first two rarely stray out of the category of "minor impairment of functioning," unless you are the one sharing a stall with a dizzy, snoring unicorn.

The third, though, has resulted numerous times in significant property damage due to tainted unicorn vomit. If you suspect one of your unicorns is dealing with acid reflux, take away his or her coffee mug and chili bowl and head to the vet.

PROPER CARE FOR SICK UNICORNS

Some breeds are sturdier than others. Karmics, for example, can get an annual flu shot every five years, preventing not only the flu but also cancer. Purebreds, on the other hand, can be a pincushion of vaccine syringes and still fall victim to every disease three times over.

Nonetheless, death is rarely an option or even a consideration for unicorns, so a farmer's attention merely needs to be placed on nursing the unicorn back to health. Because the unicorn's body has powers of expedited healing, this will likely be less than three days.

First off, it must be stated that unicorns, once removed from the wild, are not good at being sick (FIG. 7.b.). They are melodramatic and feign inability to care for themselves. You can call them on it, but this is embarrassing to them and met with extreme denial; you will then be placed on trust probation for a longer time than it is worth. Therefore, the most viable option is to discuss with the health provider the appropriateness of a steady treatment of morphine—for the unicorn, not for you.

FIGURE 7.b. *A melodramatically sick unicorn.*

If the sickness is more persistent, such as acne or bipolar disorder, the unicorn may calm down after a week because he or she, too, tires from attention-seeking antics. In the case of mental health, some unicorn farmers have found success with hiring a unicorn whisperer.

Much like a whisperer of horses, dogs, and ghosts, a unicorn whisperer communicates with the unicorn using its own language. Some unicorns respond well to this treatment, but others react poorly to the mispronunciations and improper accent of the non-native speaker. If your unicorns tend toward elitism, skip this option.

ꙮ CASE STUDY ꙮ

PEGGY AND THE WHISPERS OF FAILURE

When behavior problems became rampant among her unicorns, Peggy resolved to try out a unicorn whisperer. Out of desperation, she called the first one she found on the internet and skipped asking for references. The unicorn whisperer arrived two hours late for the appointment, and then confessed that this was her first whispering engagement. Peggy could think of no other options and allowed the unicorn whisperer to gain experience on her unicorns. Within twenty minutes, the unicorns had turned against one another, thanks to the whisperer mispronouncing one of her whispers. Peggy called the Department of Natural Resources and reported the unicorns had gone rabid. She resolved never to make another decision while desperate. Until she met her next boyfriend.

The easiest and most affordable option for an elite faction is to let the unicorns take care of each other. If one is sick, the polycorn posse can visit with the unicorn and touch its horn with theirs. Top it off with a baby's laughter, and the unicorn will be as good as new.

WISDOM FROM A RETIRED UNICORN FARMER

The touching of horns seems like an easy shortcut to health, but it only works if all members of the polycorn posse want the sick unicorn to heal. In snobby cliques, there is a bond similar to what is known in human circles as "honor among thieves." If one of their fellow unicorns is sick, they all worry about the stability of the group's status and will do everything in their power to return the situation to homeostasis. This can be used to your advantage so you don't have to pay for more morphine.

PREVENTING A UNICORN UPRISING

With the exception of the Karmics' unpredictable temper, unicorns are known by and large for their serene diplomacy. Thus, it may seem to be a surprise to you, the aspiring unicorn farmer, to see the phrase "Unicorn Uprising" in the title of this section.

Such revolutions can and do happen though, so you will want to be properly armed and prepared. To handle a mutinous unicorn follow these steps, known as the ESAH Method:

1. Establish Eye contact with the unicorn.
2. Approach Slowly but directly.

3. Extend your Arms.
4. Hug the unicorn.

The uprising will end once all unicorns have been hugged.

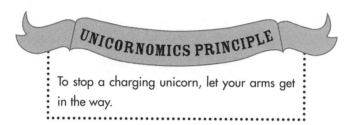

UNICORNOMICS PRINCIPLE

To stop a charging unicorn, let your arms get in the way.

Unicorn uprisings are overall quite rare, as any unicorn farmer worth his salt knows how to prevent them. A primary means of squelching an uprising while it is still zygotic is to thwart the unionization of unicorns on your farm (FIG. 7.c.).

When they were first invented, unions were meant to protect employees and improve working conditions. In the hoofs of modern unicorns, though, unions can be mutated into anarchistic coups d'état with unreasonable demands and egregious consequences.

PUT THE "UNION" BACK IN UNICORN

FIGURE 7.c. *A unicorn on strike.*

There are four stages to a unicorn unionization-turned-uprising (FIG. 7.d.).

It should come as no surprise, then, that our recommendation is to cut it off before the unicorns are cognizant of the problems. Celebrate how wonderful your farm is, and provide adequate distractions so their ADD prevents them from recognizing if there is an issue. Be generous with your resolutions, and distribute newsletters to the unicorns reminding them of recent improvements.

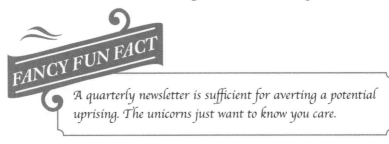

FANCY FUN FACT

A quarterly newsletter is sufficient for averting a potential uprising. The unicorns just want to know you care.

If it progresses into the Organization stage or Unionization stage, *stop telling the unicorns to get back to work.* Listen to them, take some notes, and alter some practices to make them happy. It's as simple as that. Your farm and the local townspeople will thank you.

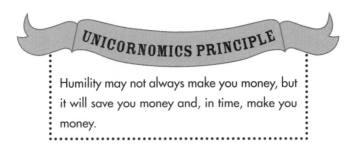

UNICORNOMICS PRINCIPLE

Humility may not always make you money, but it will save you money and, in time, make you money.

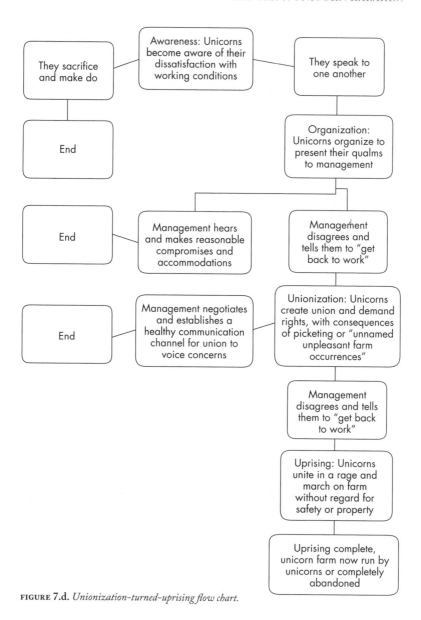

FIGURE 7.d. *Unionization-turned-uprising flow chart.*

ℰ *TESTIMONIAL* ℒ

MAI-LING AND THE THREAT OF UNICORN UNIONIZATION

As the only female unicorn farmer who supplied steeds to unicorn rodeos, Mai-Ling was one tough mama jama. However, when her unicorns discussed unionizing in protest of this high-risk employment, she was at a loss. "Working with some real scuzbags at these rodeos, I never thought it would be the *unicorns* that would make me uneasy." She decided to hear the unicorns out and give them a chance to pick ways to make themselves more comfortable with this line of work. "In the end, they just wanted the rodeo clowns gone. We replaced the clowns with a trampoline slam-dunking basketball team, and none of the audiences have really noticed. In addition, the unicorns decided they didn't want the bother of truly unionizing." It pays to listen, Mai-Ling found, and sometimes that payment comes in dollar form from not having to deal with an uprising.

TAKE IT WITH YOU!

1. Unicorns are distractible, gullible, and adorable.
2. Sick unicorns will provide discomfort to you, but if you are patient they will heal themselves quickly and not hate you.
3. Unicorns have been known to revolt on rare occasions. To be prepared for such an event, practice the ESAH method: Eye contact, Slow approach, Arms extended, Hug.
4. Unicorn unions can be squelched before they solidify through active listening and effective negotiation.

READER'S NOTES:

⁓ PART 2 ⁓
IN CONCLUSION

This section has given you a glimpse into the real lives of unicorns, helping you to become an informed consumer and caretaker. It's easier to appreciate them from a distance, but it takes a true unicorn farmer with the innate skills of protecting them, harnessing their magic, and outsmarting them to turn their quirks into cash.

Remember: Behind every unicorn that poses as an independent enigma with confidence, peace, and a carefree life, there is an exhausted unicorn farmer standing behind her, ambivalently struggling with pride and jealousy.

UNICORNOMICS PRINCIPLE

Embrace the pride, and you'll embrace the profit.

PART 3

IMPLEMENTATION

CHAPTER 8
....

DIFFERENT WAYS TO OBTAIN UNICORNS

As much as we may wish Pinocchio and his cricket pal were correct, putting your hope in a celestial body will not make unicorns appear.

At least, not in most cases.

There have been a few documented cases where, in response to an unspoken heart's desire, a unicorn has materialized out of nothing, but these tales inevitably end with the moral, "Be careful what you wish for."

This chapter will introduce you to more reliable methods for attracting, acquiring, and corralling the right unicorns.

OBTAINING CATTLE

The story is told of an elderly unicorn farmer who was approached by a young, brazen, inexperienced unicorn-farmer hopeful.

"I need your knowledge," the young man curtly announced to his aged counterpart. "I just moved from the city to open my own unicorn farm, and I hear you're the best in the business. How did you grow your farm?"

The farmer glanced at the young man and lazily munched on his red licorice rope. He looked away from his visitor in the direction of his own farm for several minutes. The young man was becoming impatient, and finally exclaimed, "How can I make unicorns come to my farm?"

The farmer turned back to him and looked him in the eye. "With a better attitude."

This is a law of unicorn farming: You must maintain the proper attitude. Whether you are a gentle breeder or are planning to create a deadly army to vanquish your enemies, unicorns can read temperaments and incongruence. And they will respond accordingly. And they will pass this information on to others.

In fact, when it comes to responding to others, unicorns are tactless creatures when conveying messages, much like a young child who hasn't yet learned that repeating Dad's comments about his boss is not appropriate dinner behavior when said manager is visiting. Unlike a child, though, the unicorn will never cultivate a filter.

But let's get back to answering the young farmer's question, which—let's be honest—the old farmer really didn't answer appropriately. The main methods for obtaining unicorns are as follows:

- Capturing them in the wild
- Buying them from another farm, zoo, or private breeder
- Accepting them as an inheritance from an eccentric mythologist's estate

Of these methods, the most preferred are capturing them or obtaining them from other farms, zoos, or breeders. Which of these paths is best for you depends on your farm's purpose and your level of laziness.

You can start a unicorn farm with a solitary animal, but the majority of farming literature recommends that you have at least two in your possession. The only exception is if you have a traveling one-unicorn show.

UNICORNS FROM THE WILD

While the unrestrained vigor can be a handful, there are many benefits to hunting and capturing your own unicorns. The most obvious benefit, of course, is that you get to observe the unicorn in its natural ecosystem. This includes the feeding, resting, and defecating that make the unicorn the numinous creature that it is.

Secondly, unicorns show appreciation for being rescued. Autumn and winter are prime hunting seasons for El Chupacabra, one of the unicorn's deadliest aggressors, so plan to swoop in and save your unicorn in the nick of time. He or she will develop an immediate loyalty to his or her rescuer (i.e., you), and will follow you anywhere.

A domesticated, spoiled unicorn—not so much.

Thirdly, wild unicorns bring new genes to the breeding pool. Incest is not a favored option in the unicorn breeding industry; therefore, wild unicorns are highly sought after. This will bring you plenty of opportunities to make extra cash when it comes to mating season options. (Be certain to include that in your business plan.)

If you cannot rescue a unicorn, you will have to trap one. This is the general procedure:

1. In order to trap a unicorn, you will need to have women on the team, as mentioned in Chapter 2.
2. Wear dust masks and goggles in case the unicorn gets spooked and shakes its mane in order to shield itself with a dust attack.
3. Be prepared with a tractor-trailer that can handle up to 3,000 pounds per unicorn (FIG. 8.a.). To accommodate the horn and the variety of heights within the species, the height of the tractor-trailer should reach at least twenty feet with holes poked in the roof, or—even better—have no roof at all.

FIGURE 8.a. *Tractor-trailer with unicorns loaded on it.*

WISDOM FROM A RETIRED UNICORN FARMER

If your unicorn handlers came from the horse industry, get them out of the habit of measuring things with hands. No one measures a unicorn with hands. Your farm will be the butt of all unicorn-farm jokes if you make this mistake. Use feet or meters. If those units are too difficult to master, avoid questions involving measuring altogether.

The least brutal way to attract a unicorn is with the no-fail virgin. If one is not on your staff, your OCV is not reachable, and no one steps forward to volunteer, then an elephant tranquilizer is the next best choice. Be sure to use a tranquilizer gun to administer the sedation.

Keep in mind that you should never approach a wild unicorn with a syringe, unless it is unconscious. *From a tranquilizer gun. From a substantial distance.* Wild unicorns are as bad as a five-year-old child when it comes to needles, and they have a lot more muscle mass from outrunning El Chupacabra.

Once the unicorn has been captured by a woman, there is no more danger of him or her losing his or her magic to a man. That means you can use male virgins anytime after the unicorn has been put into the tractor-trailer. You may not ever have this opportunity presented to you, as hiring a male virgin is often much more expensive than hiring a female virgin, and there are high rates of turnover.

When it comes to unloading the unicorn and leading him or her into a stall, plan to use a blindfold, not blinders (FIG. 8.b.). Unicorns do not have a direct X-ray line-of-sight, but they do have X-ray peripheral vision. Use the blindfold to keep them dependent on you. The blindfold should be placed over the unicorn's eyes while the unicorn is distracted by shiny baubles and trinkets in the trailer, and it can be removed once the unicorn is safely in the stall.

To assist in the transition from freedom to captivity, attempt to replicate the ecosystem from which you removed the animal (FIG. 8.c.). A typical unicorn ecosystem consists of:

FIGURE 8.b. *A blindfold commonly used for unicorns.*

- Endless blue sky with cotton candy clouds
- Double rainbows raining diamonds
- Emerald-green grass, soft as a baby's lock of hair
- Sapphire-blue pond, clear as a smog-free Los Angeles
- Centaurs, cherubs, and seahorses for playtime
- Moss and leaves for mealtime (add raw meat for the Karmics and wadded-up tissues for the Gigglerumps)
- Open meadow full of blooming flowers for exercise
- Brown tree bark on which to rub his or her face and sharpen his or her horn
- Fine-grade sand in which to bury his or her excrement
- A cardboard cutout of El Chupacabra (used only when the unicorn is naughty and needs a healthy dose of fear drilled into him or her)

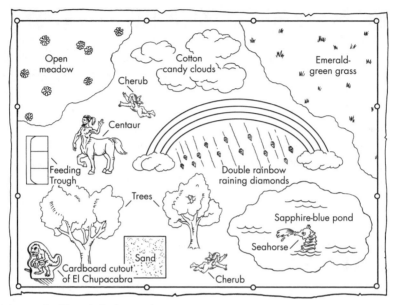

FIGURE 8.c. *The typical unicorn ecosystem.*

Your wild unicorns will demonstrate considerable vivacity, the benefit of not getting them from domesticated stock. This power and ambition will result in great energy for tasks on the farm, as well as lively stage shows.

At first, though, a unicorn may exhibit some aggression and disorientation as he or she becomes accustomed to the new surroundings. Give him or her space to explore, and don't be afraid to use some disciplinary techniques to teach limits. To avoid the wrath of animal rights groups and fantasy fiction fanatics, it is best that you know and practice the difference between discipline and punishment.

DISCIPLINE VS. PUNISHMENT	
DISCIPLINE	PUNISHMENT
A time-out of ten minutes for bad behavior	Holding the unicorn's head underwater for ten minutes for bad behavior
A gentle but abrupt tap on the snout to get his or her attention	Punching his or her nose because "You deserve it"
Giving him or her a choice of consequences: no ambrosia dessert, or no playtime in the simulated enchanted forest	Taking away dessert and playtime for the rest of his or her life, with frequent references to the unicorn being "a disappointment"

UNICORNS FROM FARMS, ZOOS, AND BREEDERS

Domestication dulls the senses. Wild unicorns now residing in confinement know this fact all too well (FIG. 8.d.). So opt for second-generation unicorns. They are less despondent and do not waste time pining for "the good old days."

Many farmers prefer domesticated unicorns because the farmer does not have the resources or patience to train a wild unicorn. In addition, these domesticated unicorns are the best

FIGURE 8.d. *A wild unicorn who is not happy with his new confinement.*

for petting zoos or any other activity that requires a display of the loss of willpower.

✎ *TESTIMONIAL* ✎

EMMET'S SUCCESSFUL DEPRESSION

"I had originally wanted to own a real zoo, where the animals were brought in from the wild and still had some kind of spark." This is Emmet's opening line as he takes visitors on a tour of his multibillion-dollar unicorn, pegasus, griffin, chimera, wyvern, and jabberwocky petting zoo. When it came to hunting and capturing unicorns, Emmet had neither the guile nor the patience to go after wild unicorns. He accepted this limitation and instead invested in domesticated cattle. It was during the Mediocre Depression, when selling mythological livestock was particularly challenging and numerous sellers gave Emmet drastically high discounts on their creatures. He smiles at the thought. "I guess some kinds of depression can lead to making lots of money!"

The key to successful negotiations with your unicorn source is making certain that the unicorn you are acquiring has minimal liability and maximum potential. No small price tag will make up for major behavioral issues or medical bills.

What should you look for when identifying a potential candidate for your farm?

UNICORN APPEARANCE EVALUATION

FEATURE	HEALTHY	SICKLY
Eyes	Immediately attentive; white sclera; iris color appropriate to breed (see table in Chapter 2)	Delayed reaction; blood-shot or jaundiced sclera; red iris (unless Karmic, which exhibits no iris when ill); crust around eyelids
Coat	Shiny; smooth; glittery; sending out rays of sunshine and hope	Missing
Hoofs	Horse-like hoofs; solid; a scent of lavender when stepping	Fused; splintered; sulfuric odor
Horn	Shape appropriate to breed; solid	Flaking; mushy
Posture (FIG. 8.e.)	Standing tall; confident; balanced	Head unable to be lifted past shoulders; buttocks dragging on ground; asymmetrical
Gait	Measured; consistent; graceful	Clunky; not using all legs
General Demeanor	Pleasant; adheres to routine; responsive; friendly toward innocent children with hearts full of wonder	Irritability without cessation; lethargic; disoriented; circadian rhythms arrhythmic; targets any human shorter than 4 feet

FIGURE 8.e. *(From left) Healthy unicorn; sick unicorn.*

Once you have inspected the unicorn to determine his or her bill of health, you can make your statement of negotiation.

Keep in mind, before entering into any situation where you may end up taking home a unicorn, you should know your intentions. If you do not know your fiscal goals and limits, discuss these ahead of time with a financial advisor who does not think purchasing a unicorn is an act of certifiable insanity.

Another option is to barter for your unicorn. Acceptable items of trade include food, services, and ceramic jars labeled "eye of newt." Other items are situation-dependent, so you should do some research before meeting to barter. For example, one well-known breeder has an avid interest in vintage tiki masks, and a popular Eastern-European zoo has been blackmailed numerous times into giving away animals.

UNICORNS FROM INHERITANCE

The third way to obtain a unicorn is to receive one as a gift or an inheritance (FIG. 8.f.). This does not involve any exchange on your part, but instead simply receiving the animal into your care. It is in poor taste to refuse a gift, and it is very difficult to turn down an inheritance, so it is a wise plan to always be prepared to receive a unicorn. This is especially true if you have an eccentric elderly relative prone to unusual hoarding behaviors and frequent acquisition trips to exotic lands.

FIGURE 8.f. *A unicorn who was given as a birthday gift.*

Whichever option you prefer (or have forced upon you), do your part to prepare ahead of time.

- Become knowledgeable regarding unicorn features and behavior that will provide indicators as to the creature's value.
- Engage in regular market analysis of unicorn worth and competitors' pricing.
- Evaluate your own capabilities and capacity so you aren't swayed into a wacky impulse buy.

With this preparation and planning, you can advance into the next step: assembling your unicorn farm.

UNICORNOMICS PRINCIPLE

A plan to win is a plan for winners!

ஃ *CASE STUDY* ஃ

AHMED'S LESS SUCCESSFUL DEPRESSION

Ahmed bought cattle during the Mediocre Depression. However, he did not realize what he was getting and attempted to prompt the domesticated unicorns to behave as those from the wild. Like socialites invited to a tractor pull, the unicorns turned up their delicate snouts and returned to sleeping, bathing, and having their manes braided. Ahmed's customers grew bored watching the unicorns primp, and they took their wild-unicorn-related business elsewhere. Ahmed sold his remaining unicorns to Emmet's multibillion-dollar petting zoo.

TAKE IT WITH YOU!

1. There are many ways to accumulate unicorns, but your main concern should be whether you want wild or domesticated unicorns.
2. Wild unicorns may be more active and interesting, but they tend to be renegades.
3. Domesticated unicorns may be more agreeable and easily satisfied, but they tend to be lazy.
4. Catching a wild unicorn involves women, dust masks, a tractor-trailer, and either a virgin or a tranquilizer gun.
5. A unicorn benefits from an ecosystem that mirrors what he or she thinks nature should look like.
6. Before purchasing a unicorn, examine his or her appearance for health and magical well-being.

READER'S NOTES:

_____

_____

_____

_____

_____

_____

_____

_____

CHAPTER 9

THE FARM

It should go without saying that unicorns can be high-maintenance. There is a popular saying that is muttered throughout the unicorn farming community:

If you want a hole in your wallet, use a unicorn's horn.

With this stereotype of the high-maintenance unicorn in mind, it is time to address the topic of the environment. First and foremost, keep the unicorn comfortable and safe. A unicorn in danger is unpleasant, but a unicorn in discomfort is a terror.

Plan for your unicorn farm to include the elements listed in the ecosystem earlier in this manual. If yours are second-generation domesticated unicorns, you can cheat a bit with this. For example, instead of a shining sapphire pond, you can use an enlarged puddle that has been dyed blue with food coloring. Also, you will not need to rely on centaurs or cherubs because second-generation unicorns are more open-minded about their social circle.

When it comes to farm equipment, unicorns are spooked by loud noises, so it is preferable to use old-timey implements. After all, it is difficult to find modern apparatuses that have been inspected for safe use around this brand of cattle. Scythes, hand-held shears, and push lawnmowers maintain a tranquil environment while getting your farm work done in only four to five times the amount of time.

For a good deal, look for stores that stock the Ye Olde-Fashioned Farm Tool Kit (FIG. 9.a). It will have all the equipment you need. If you are a high roller when it comes to your farming paraphernalia, check out the Ye Olde-Fashioned Deluxe Farm Tool Kit, as well as the massive assortment of novelty add-ons. Some of the most popular add-ons in the frivolous spendthrift category are rhinestones for

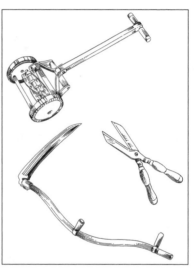

FIGURE 9.a. *Tools included in the Ye Olde-Fashioned Farm Tool Kit.*

shear blades, spinners for spinning wheels, and heated seats for unicorn-drawn plows.

The ideal layout of your farm will provide adequate walking and running room, high ceilings, spacious stalls, nature or faux nature, and toys for mental stimulation so the unicorns do not grow bored.

You must also take into account the needs of your visitors and customers. One element that many novice unicorn farmers often overlook is a stable map (FIG. 9.b.). This map provides an overview of the layout of your unicorn stables, ensuring that a wandering visitor will not meander into a temperamental Karmic's stall or an occupied mating room.

WISDOM FROM A RETIRED UNICORN FARMER

If you plan to make your fortune selling unicorn milk, you will have a highly receptive and loyal market. You will also have a big problem on your hands if you plan to use a catheter milking system. It did not go over well with cows in the mid-1800s, and it has not gained any love with unicorns of today. Hand milking will keep the peace between you and your unicorn-milk source. The bottom line: Old-timey need not mean primitive, just inefficient.

Unicorn boredom is a dangerous disease for the profit-driven farmer. Unicorns whose brains are not regularly engaged in activities often lose their luster and their color, which will cause anything they produce to drastically decline in value. Therefore, set a line item in your budget to invest extensively and shamelessly in tools for mental stimulation (i.e., oversized toys).

Unless you are struck by a lightning bolt of good fortune, your unicorn will indeed be high-maintenance and these tools will be the most expensive of all the equipment on your farm. To start, then, plan to purchase 50 percent of what you need and use activities to replace the other 50 percent. Here are some examples of general starter toys and activities.

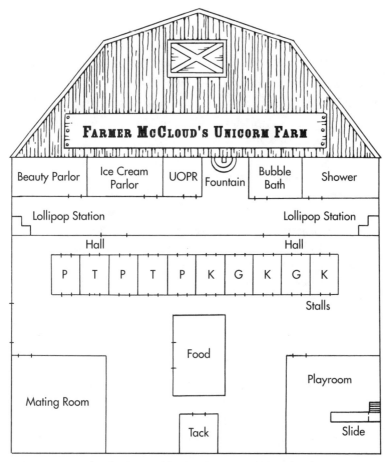

P = Purebred   T = Twinkletoe   K = Karmic   G = Gigglerump
UOPR = Unicorn-Only Powder Room

FIGURE 9.b. *A stable map.*

GENERAL STARTER TOYS AND ACTIVITIES FOR UNICORNS

TOYS FOR MENTAL STIMULATION	ACTIVITIES
Pilate balls	Swimming
Bubbles	Ring toss on the alicorn
Supersized Connect Four	Bocce ball
A marble hidden in a boot	Tetherball
Pinball	Chess (for all but Gigglerumps)
Jungle gym with monster truck–tire swings, hanging-chain "jiggle" bridges, and slides reinforced with steel girders	King of the Mountain (especially for Karmics)

Note that leapfrog is not on the activities list.

For the most part, Purebred and Twinkletoe unicorns enjoy team sports, particularly those in which everybody wins, or if that isn't possible, where the fewest players lose. Karmics are the inverse of that, and Gigglerumps just want an "I participated in having fun!" ribbon (FIG. 9.c.).

FIGURE 9.c. *A Gigglerump who has just played a game.*

A major factor that you should consider in your farm's layout is safety. You will need to protect your unicorns from visitors (if your farm is open to the public), each other, and their natural enemies. The natural enemies of the unicorn are:

- El Chupacabra
- Philip Seymour Hoffman

El Chupacabra is easy to detect and prepare against, but Philip Seymour Hoffman is a bit sneakier. Seek out Philip Seymour Hoffman Repellant from your nearest obscure novelty shop.

WARNING: In many rural areas, unicorn tipping is a popular late-night pastime for the youth and must be actively guarded against. A tipped unicorn is a vengeful unicorn.

While dragons, chimera, zombies, and minotaurs are sometimes labeled as enemies of the unicorn, they are merely nuisances. This also goes for various individuals of literature and lore who dine on chosen aspects of the unicorn; the unicorns understand that rarely is it an issue of cruelty as much as it is one of sustenance or poetic license. Of course, as with all nuisances, there is a spectrum of intensity, and dragons often fall on the "full-out frustration" end due to their neediness, frequent mood swings, and poor breathing habits.

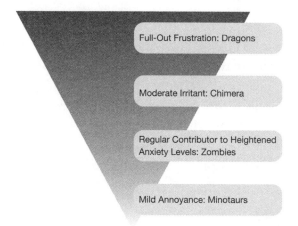

Full-Out Frustration: Dragons

Moderate Irritant: Chimera

Regular Contributor to Heightened Anxiety Levels: Zombies

Mild Annoyance: Minotaurs

There is also an ongoing but friendly battle with the narwhal. When a unicorn is able to make his or her way to the ocean, a visit to this horned sea mammal is often in order. Using only their horns, the unicorn and narwhal battle sans gloves and rules. While this combat can lead to fierce impalements for both sides, it usually ends with a truce that involves the losing party buying the other a beer and talking about the good ol' days.

FANCY FUN FACT

A unicorn can have a beer from time to time, but anything beyond 9 percent alcohol will inevitably lead to dancing with a lampshade on his or her horn. If you tire easily of intoxicated animals and worn-out-drunken-behavior clichés, keep the unicorns' imbibing to a minimum.

The last consideration for layout involves the purpose of your farm. Will it be open to the public, or will it only serve as the center of production and distribution? For example, if you plan to open a depot for the Unicorn Express at your farm, you will need to consult with OSHA to determine if your facilities are equally human-compatible. On the other hand, if visitors will not be welcomed on the grounds, you can design your farm to exhibit more of a "pigsty-chic" atmosphere.

OPENING THE FARM

Because it is up to you to decide the particular focus of your farm, this section will address only the basics to assist you in getting your unicorn farm up and running.

When you finally make your farm happen, it's a big day. It could simply be the day that you walk through the doors and yell at the unicorns to stop being lazy, or it may be the Grand Opening Bonanza that the entire metropolis has been reading about in the local newspaper for weeks (FIG. 9.d.).

FIGURE 9.d. *A local newspaper headline deservedly celebrating a unicorn farm grand opening.*

To guarantee the opening of your farm is timely and appropriate, know your product and your audience. It will take more time to prepare and open a farm that has extensive and expensive laboratory facilities for purifying unicorn feces than it will for a unicorn farm that serves only as an acorn factory.

Remember: You don't have to have the coolest opening or the quickest start-up, but it helps!

Public Openings

For public openings, the primary objectives are to set a date and procure lots of confetti. Also, establish some awesome giveaways and door prizes. These can be unicorn-based calendars (FIG. 9.e.), combs, bumper stickers, pens, bottle openers, or plush dolls with shoddy stitching. They will typically include the name and contact information for said farm, as well as a corny slogan:

FIGURE 9.e. *A unicorn-based calendar.*

- "Where magic comes alive!"
- "I brake for horns and glitter!"
- "Hoof it over to Farmer McCormick's Unicornicopia!"

Notice that all of these statements end in an exclamation point. That conveys excitement. Remember this rule of marketing:

The more exclamation points that you use, the more excited your guests will be about your product!!!!!

Be conservative in the use of the series exclamation points, however. You should never have more exclamation points than letters in the statement preceding the punctuation. Consider an average of three exclamation points per statement until you strike your copy-writing groove.

Mark the cheapest items as giveaways, and the more expensive items as door prizes. While neither should cost you more than $5.00, you will find everyone from children on tricycles to full-grown, chauffeured executives fighting for possession of these goodies. This is called *supply and demand*. Create *demand* by having only a few items as door prizes during the opening, and a limited *supply* of the same items in the gift shop at an absurdly high markup. This generates a false sense of value, magnetizing your guests to your branding and, therefore, your product.

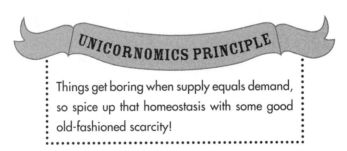

UNICORNOMICS PRINCIPLE

Things get boring when supply equals demand, so spice up that homeostasis with some good old-fashioned scarcity!

✣ *CASE STUDY* ✣
EMMY LOU'S NOT-SO-SURE THING

With a name that innately aligned her with a farmer's life, Emmy Lou bought her unicorn farm with dollar signs practically engraved on her pupils. She had an MBA, a business plan, and a template for an annual report. No one in the history of unicorn farming had been more prepared. Emmy Lou's first step in opening her unicorn farm was to open the gift shop, at which she established a currency consisting of "Unicorn Bux." She only sold these in two Bux denominations, since solitary Bux were confusing in their plural title. This ultimately led to the shop's downfall, as customers were frustrated with the inability to receive exact change and eventually instituted a permanent boycott.

Private Openings

If your opening is a private affair, send out notices to the locals that your product or service will be available soon. Don't forget to indicate where it will be made available. Then open the door and get to work.

Not as glamorous as a public opening, eh? Then maybe you should reconsider your business plan.

Because people love grand openings and free stuff.

MAINTAINING THE FARM

The grand opening may be a blast, but the actual farm day-to-day maintenance takes work. Hard, boring work. You will need to handle advertising, finances, health concerns, contracts, employee relations, etc.

Therefore, you have two choices if you want to be successful: Either plan to be responsible and take action on the realities of owning this farm and caring for these creatures in your custody, or have another grand opening!

Obviously, grand openings have much more to offer everyone, including the unicorns, who get freakishly excited at the sight of streamers, balloons, and bright colors (FIG. 9.f.).

Nevertheless, if you insist on demonstrating maturity in your business decisions, plan

FIGURE 9.f. *A deliriously delighted unicorn at a grand opening.*

to work toward your goals in concrete, measurable ways. Focus on customer relations, track data, limit liabilities, stay confident in your pricing, stay competitive, increase exposure, etc.

Seriously, grand openings are *so* much better.

GROWING YOUR FARM

"How can I grow my farm?"

Like the cocky young aspiring farmer in Chapter 8, many unicorn farmers find themselves asking this question. Recent research by several independent unicorn-farm consulting firms have revealed that this is the second most common question related to unicorn farming, the first being, "Do unicorns exist?"

Growth comes in a variety of forms. The form you choose is based on your initial reason for dreaming of this farm. The major growth forms are expanded networking, greater distribution, increased cattle population, improved animated-neon displays, and new goals. In addition, at the end of this chapter, you will learn how to gain some critical reconnaissance regarding the opening of distribution channels of which you are currently unaware because your competition has been hogging them all.

WARNING: In the mystical creature business, stealing ideas can have grave consequences based on your chosen creature's symbolism. Griffins symbolize power, so they will applaud your shrewdness with your high-status approach. But you don't own a griffin farm. And a unicorn is the poster child for purity. If you opt for underhanded ploys, do not let on to what you are doing unless you have your unicorns' undying loyalty. (They *will* eventually see through your scheme, but blind loyalty paves over all kinds of transgressions.)

If you choose to gather your market information through more socially acceptable means, pat yourself on the back for earning a Boy Scout badge in integrity. Unfortunately, that badge earns you nothing when it comes to the business world, so get out some spreadsheets (FIG. 9.g.).

Write down some convincing numbers that you have gleaned from analyzing your overhead, profit margin, and other compelling business lingo; then confidently state to your shareholders, stakeholders, employees, or anyone else who will listen to a speech about unicorn profitability that you are going to access an untapped market.

FIGURE 9.g. *Sparkling spreadsheets.*

The great thing about untapped markets is that they tend to be so obscure that you do not have to have a legitimate reason for chasing after them. People are merely impressed that you are aware that they exist.

If you do happen to be questioned on your reasoning, it is easy to come up with a loosely constructed explanation of the correlation of your sales to the success of the population in question. Besides, you are working with unicorns. Who can honestly ask if you know what you are doing?

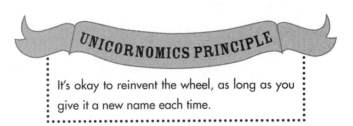

UNICORNOMICS PRINCIPLE

It's okay to reinvent the wheel, as long as you give it a new name each time.

MARKETING YOUR FARM

No matter how amazing you think your business may be, you will need to work to get the word out eventually and perpetually. This usually costs quite a bit of money for advertisements and attention-grabbing activities, as well as employing a full-time specialist to deal with public relations, which typically consists of sending out press releases then jumping up and down trying to get the stingy attention of the media.

While these methods are traditional and reliable, they are losing relevance in today's novelty-saturated marketplace. In recent years, some unicorn farmers have discovered another way.

If you are of the mindset that any publicity is good publicity, this new approach may be of interest to you. It involves dramatic acts that draw attention and consequently, the media. For example, one unicorn farmer blew up an old empty barn on her property and blamed it on a nonexistent hooligan; by the time the hooligan's name was confirmed to be false, the farmer was a celebrity. She now has a syndicated-radio talk show, an advice column in a national business publication, and is writing a tell-all memoir.

To take this approach, there is risk involved, other than safety. For example, if you manage the public's attention poorly, you may lose it. The key is to grasp it immediately, recognizing that curiosity, not quality, will bring in potential customers. You have the opportunity to convert them to real customers once they arrive, and that is when you confront them with your high-quality services and wares. To do so prematurely, though, comes off as desperate in this circumstance.

Another risk is that your livestock find out. But that dead unicorn has already been beaten enough in this chapter.

Lastly, you risk the name of the culprit becoming bigger than the business. If you are the fall guy or gal, keep your ego in check and keep bringing it back to the business. If you have used a scapegoat or scapeunicorn, brief and debrief her on the superficial purpose of this "marketing opportunity," reminding her that you will be the spokesperson to keep her from getting confused. This should keep you in control while she feels noble for her contributions.

✒ TESTIMONIAL ✑

BENJAMIN THE GUERRILLA MARKETER

Having read about guerrilla marketing in the newspaper after dropping out of college, Benjamin knew how to attract attention with little investment. It was a good thing, too, since he had spent all of his money buying unicorns. Staging a flash mob that involved all of his friends and their friends dressing as unicorns, they met at the town hall and danced to Peter, Paul, and Mary's folk anthem "The Unicorn Song." "The recording quality was pretty bad and the song was tough to choreograph to, but the mere presence of seventy-two grown adults prancing as unicorns seemed to have a pretty impressive impact on everybody around," he reports. During the next few weeks, Benjamin enjoyed appearances in local newspapers and fame throughout the country. He is now pursuing a career as a unicorn-marketing coach. "I'll be the only one in the business — it's a pretty good corner on the market."

Of course, a successful business drawing attention will create competition. Your farm may be the only one of its type for several thousand miles, but you can count on people wanting to cash in on your fiscal influx. Their unicorns may neither be real nor their barn walls free of asbestos, but these individuals will work hard to make your corner on the market their personal space, too.

Many new farmers wish to avoid competition. This is a misunderstanding of the purpose of a competitor. A competitor is not an evil arch-nemesis who studies your every move to eventually torture and assassinate you. In fact, during the past five years, assassinations related to competition among farmers of mythical livestock have been at an all-time low.

Competitors simply want your money, so they will pull all kinds of wacky hijinks to get that money away from you. You, in turn, can capitalize on their bad ideas and develop your identity as the antithesis to their inferior craftsmanship, performance, or facilities.

UNICORNOMICS PRINCIPLE

Use your competition like the slimming mirror in a department store in a dimly lit fitting room: to make you look better, inducing more sales.

INSIDERS' KNOWLEDGE

When gaining an inside scoop on your competition's business strategies, resist the urge to do the spying on your own. Instead, consider these options:

- Read the news regarding market trends
- Hire a business consultant to improve your productivity and quality
- Send a Trojan Unicorn (FIG. 9.h.)

The Trojan Unicorn is clearly the most attractive choice on this list. If you believe that your competitor will take in a large unicorn on wheels without questioning it, then it is in your best interest to take advantage of that gullibility.

When creating this decoy, do not use a real unicorn carcass. You will be reviled in the unicorn community if any other farmers catch wind of this decision. And they will—gossip travels quickly amongst the unfiltered. Instead, use a blanket or burlap sacks

FIGURE 9.h. *A Trojan Unicorn.*

sutured together and shaped into a four-legged horned mammal. For added impact, a plastic Halloween mask is often effective.

You will need to load the creature full of recording devices, so have the stomach hollowed out to accommodate these items. If you have a gadget genius on your team—and it is worthwhile to invest in one, should you have the capital—request that the eyes be linked to the camera and controlled by remote. The purpose of this is that the scheme sounds much cooler if you can think of your Trojan Unicorn as a robot.

Of course, do not expect to get the decoy back. If your competitor discovers that it is a spying mechanism, you can expect some kind of legal action for your team of lawyers, or at the very least, a public besmirching of your reputation. And, if your competitor does not make this discovery, he will continue to assume it is part of their livestock.

Just let it go in the name of progress. Synergy!

UNICORNOMICS PRINCIPLE

If plans go askew and you end up with a trade embargo against your farm, send the opposing forces baskets of cupcakes, candy, and friendship bracelets to restore order in the unicorn universe.

TAKE IT WITH YOU!

1. When it comes to farm equipment, old-timey is sublimcy for unicorns' peace of mind.
2. Prevent unicorn boredom with toys, games, activities, and shiny objects.
3. Always be on guard to defend your unicorns against El Chupacabra and Philip Seymour Hoffman; unicorns can often deal with the less malevolent characters themselves.
4. Grand openings ought to be done strategically and frequently.
5. To grow your farm, convince investors that you deserve more money. Spreadsheets are helpful in this process.
6. Trojan Unicorns are fun to make and effective at spying on the competition.

READER'S NOTES:

_____

_____

_____

_____

_____

_____

_____

_____

_____

_____

➳ PART 3 ❧
IN CONCLUSION

Getting your farm launched is an exciting time, but keeping the unicorns content is a fine art that takes a lifetime to master. To avoid the farm ownership and maintenance becoming complete drudgery, keep the fun tap on full blast at all times! Then prepare to drink in—nay, chug—the sweetness of success that comes pouring out from it.

But *always* remember to keep the unicorns comfortable so that magic flares and tempers do not.

PART 4

DIAGNOSING SUCCESS

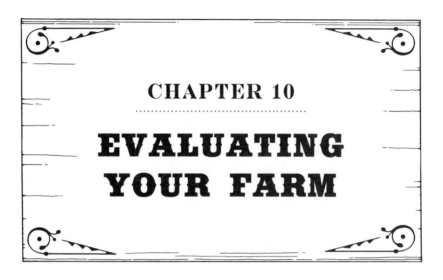

CHAPTER 10

EVALUATING YOUR FARM

What is your end goal? Pulling in the cash, hand over fist? Providing a safe haven for unicorns to live and love freely? Becoming the world's top-producing source of unicorn-horn poison control systems?

Evaluation is the step in business development that gets you to realize that you have met your goal and it's time to celebrate, or you haven't met your goal, and you are failing in one area of your life.

It's a long road to get to this point, and many farms never reach it. If you are asking yourself, "What can I do better?" then rest assured you were born to be a revolutionary unicorn farmer.

But revolutions don't happen overnight.

Well, most don't.

At least the ones that involve industry.

You started with a strategy, then implemented it and tested it out in reality. Did it work out for you? What adjustments need to be made to increase the dividends of joy and other, more tangible products of your business? These questions are what this Evaluation chapter will address.

A farm is no good if it is only breaking even. Unless that is part of your mission statement.

METRICS

Earlier in this manual, it was mentioned that you should track data. Hopefully you took that suggestion, because you will really need it here.

Data gives you numbers so you can create impressive tables and graphs with color coding and attention-grabbing shapes. Pie charts are of particular interest to the data-hungry community, and you can endear yourself to such individuals by referring to these charts as "unicorn pie." Investors love that kind of humor, and they will promptly get out their pens to write more checks upon your use of it.

Data doesn't just exist to impress others, though. That is *most* of its purpose, but not all of it. Data also gives you numbers that you can point to as you declare that you are moving forward with your mission statement.

For example, maybe you did lousily this year. You can point to the numbers and say, "These numbers are bad. We will have better numbers next year." You will then look at the numbers and how they became bad. This is called *analysis*.

Often, if you have bad numbers, it is worthwhile to show a picture of one of your cutest acorns (FIG. 10.a.). This will create a tender reaction in your audience, which is great if you have further bad news. If that is the case, have a short video on hand of the adorable acorn attempting to walk for the first time. You will earn emotional bonus points if the mother unicorn gently licks the acorn's forehead.

From there, you can use the numbers that you *do* have to determine the numbers that you *want* to have. This is called *planning*.

FIGURE 10.a. *A picture of a distractingly darling acorn and her mother to counterbalance bad numbers.*

℘ *CASE STUDY* ℘

CURT MESSES UP BIG TIME

It was his big break — a meeting with investors from across the globe. Curt had prepared some convincing presentations with percentage signs, tables, and exclamation points. Stumbling through his introduction, though, he could already sense that he was losing the crowd, so he went to his emergency acorn photo and turned to the audience to catch their reaction. The discomfort he saw was rather unanticipated. When Curt turned back to the screen, he was met with an enlarged version of the photo of thrush he had copied from a medical reference guide for self-diagnosis. He ended the meeting immediately and noted to himself that he would do a full final review of his next presentation.

Lastly, you can figure out how to help those good, wanted numbers to happen more easily. That is called *ensuring success*. Synergy!

Here are suggestions of measurable outcomes for your unicorn business:

- **Revenue:** Amount of money you have made from selling unicorns, unicorn merchandise, or unicorn consulting services
- **Customer Satisfaction:** Repeat business; frequency, volume, quality of hate mail
- **Employee Satisfaction:** Average amount of time between hire date and termination date; questionnaires assessing likelihood of each employee returning to work the next day
- **Unicorn Satisfaction:** Number of sick days; number of unicorn attacks on visitors and staff
- **Advertising Effectiveness:** Response to new ads and ad channels; number of posters and fliers that are not defaced
- **Quality of Product:** Testing results for durability; frequency of return of product for refund or exchange; percentage of lawsuits that do not involve the phrase "compromising safety"
- **Quality of Service:** Frequency of clients leaving during the course of service delivery; surveys of likelihood of referring service to a loved one; surveys of likelihood of referring service to an unloved one
- **Fanbase:** Frequency and volume of contact from fans; requests for appearances at sci-fi conventions and Renaissance festivals

Once you determine which of these metrics impact and reflect on your business, you can scrounge up some numbers and see if you did an adequate job. Then make a really cool unicorn pie to demonstrate how you will do better next time.

For those seeking a standardized measurement system, the most popular is the Unicorn Richter Scale (fig. 10.b.), established by Charles Richter twelve years earlier than his popular earthquake scale. This is used to measure the all-around impact of your unicorns.

FIGURE 10.b. *The Unicorn Richter Scale*

GATHERING DATA

Researchers make data sound easy to find, as if it is playing hide-and-seek and giggling so the seeker doesn't even have to try because of course it's hiding in the refrigerator box; because the refrigerator box isn't laughing on its own.

But that is not how data comes about. There is no laughter, and trying *is* part of the game. And that game is not hide-and-seek.

Gathering data regarding customers can occur through focus groups, cold calling during dinnertime, and questionnaires that only work as effectively as the person who designed them.

Gathering data regarding your unicorn business not only can be done by reading bank-account statements, but also keeping personal accounts in your own anal-retentive journal. Look for entries that begin with, "Today, I was on the radio," or "A unicorn compromised safety last night," or "There was a strike by my employees this week." These can be especially helpful in your research.

If you have any sentient unicorns amidst your livestock, consider asking them if they have any anecdotal evidence to share regarding business performance. Be cautious in collecting this data, though, as unicorns tend toward hyperbole in their descriptions.

Another important source of information is market analysis. Of course, a recurrent complaint of professionals in this industry is that no professional journals exist specific to unicorn businesses. Instead, examine related magazines, individual consulting-firms' research papers, information on other types of farming, and sales pertaining to unicorn novelty items. When the numbers regarding these factors are on the rise, you can expect that this is a good time to put up your best billboard (FIG. 10.c.) (or poster-board, if this fiscal year's budget does not cover highway signage).

As always, do your best to put all the information down in numerical form. Statistics are fascinating to the general population, so you can usually get by with some soft estimates. However, if that fussy data-driven investor from Chapter 4 is still involved, you may need some real numbers. Be armed with a spreadsheet of some kind with numbers you can defend. For everyone else, slice up that unicorn pie and stick a photo of your best acorn in the background.

FIGURE 10.c. *A billboard for Farmer McCloud's Unicorn Farm.*

❧ *TESTIMONIAL* ☙

OMAR MEETS DESTINEE

"Math was never my strong suit, but I knew that owning a business would require some number crunching," Omar says with a shrug. He borrowed a book from the library called *Statistics Don't Suck That Much — Really!* and identified some statistics he could monitor at his unicorn farm. While working at the local coffee shop with his spreadsheets, an attractive woman noticed his data analysis and struck up a conversation with him on the merits of math, metrics, and mocha lattes. Her name was Destinee and she was a visiting professor of Arithmetic and Math Sciences at the public university. "She couldn't believe I wasn't turned off by her life's passion — I was totally in!" Two years later, they were married.

Here is a trick for any negotiation wherein you need to face some big budget bigwig who may call your bluff: When you enter the conversation, have two statements in mind. One is a point on which you are willing to negotiate, and the other is a point on which you are not. Pretend as if both are non-negotiable. If and when the other party pushes, act reluctant, but eventually make a minor concession on the former point. But stand firm on the latter! It will look as though you are wise enough to know when to compromise, but confident enough to stand your ground and not completely cave.

Why is this trick so important? Because it is your dream, gosh-darnit! And there are unicorns involved! And no greedy hoity-toity investor can take that from you! But investors *can* take their money from you, so this trick solves that issue.

So act confident, and the scent of fake confidence (which smells strikingly similar to genuine confidence) will follow.

UNICORNOMICS PRINCIPLE

When in doubt, don't cash out!

TAKE IT WITH YOU!

1. Unicorn pie is a great way to show off your farm's statistics, or at least your graphic-design skills.
2. Everyone loves adorable acorns.
3. Identify measurable outcomes and keep track of data associated with them as you go along. This will make reporting a lot easier—and more honest.
4. Always act confident. It attracts the opposite sex, investors, and cash flow.

READER'S NOTES:

_____

_____

_____

_____

_____

_____

_____

_____

_____

_____

_____

_____

CHAPTER 11

IDEAS FOR IMPROVEMENT

So how will you do better next time? The investors and others affected by your business will want an answer to this question. It would be good if you too are interested in it.

This chapter will provide you with the creative kindling to start your own unicorn-business fire. (The preceding statement was not intended to encourage nor condone arson for the purpose of insurance-money collection.)

IDEAS

First of all, get your numbers-tracking gear on. As one hapless unicorn farmer observed, "There is no time like Year Two to fix a big boo-boo!" Make Year Two your time to address the gaping gashes in your system. You can use the suggestions for areas of assessment from Chapter 10, or allow them to stimulate your creative measurement–brain lobe.

Secondly, visualize the word "Improvement." Experience it. Own it. Listen to what it is saying to you. If after a few minutes it still hasn't talked, then just keep reading into the next section.

IMPROVEMENT

What have others done to improve their farms and boost sales after their evaluation phase? The answers below are situation-specific and completely dependent on the particular farm's strengths and weaknesses, but wouldn't it be fantastic if one of them happens to fit your particular quandary? Answer: Yes.

- Utilizing the uber-popularized art of feng shui in redesigning the farm layout to ease Karmic tantrums
- Attaining one's own Juris Doctor degree to cut down on excessive legal fees paid to lawyers on retainer
- Bedazzling the Gigglerumps to entice handlers to spend more time grooming and feeding them (FIG. 11.a.)
- Offering customers membership in an exclusive fee-based club that has rewards that are only earned once several thousand dollars have been spent

FIGURE 11.a. *A Gigglerump, decked out with rhinestones.*

- Building a giant furnace for instant cremation to cut down on the stench of the dead
- Going from private ownership to being publicly traded on NYSE under hilarious-to-pronounce stock symbol UNIC

⚮ *TESTIMONIAL* ⚮

GASPER & GERTRUDE:
EDUCATION WAS THE SECRET INGREDIENT

Married for forty-five years, Gertrude and Gasper were the cutest couple their customers had ever seen, but their bookkeeping was a mess since neither of them had attended school beyond the ninth grade. "I knew we needed some book learnin', so I took the hit and went back to school," Gasper says as he looks lovingly at his adoring wife. The long nights and weekends of writing papers paid off a few years later when Gasper walked across the stage to receive his PhD in biochemistry. "I kinda lost track of why I was at school, but I discovered that I really liked all them organisms — especially nucleic acids. I *love* nucleic acids." Gertrude took an adult-education course in accounting and has managed the books ever since, while her husband has opened up a research facility to study the synthesis of magic within the DNA of unicorns.

UNICORNOMICS PRINCIPLE

If you are breaking even, imposing a "magic tax" on purchases can increase your profit margin.

Some farms have elected to close, but that is an ill-advised decision until at least the fifth year. It typically takes a minimum of five years for a new venture to turn a profit, and it may take even longer when the venture has not previously existed in your region's awareness of possibilities. Unicorns don't sell themselves, and they shouldn't. That would be inappropriate for their reputation of purity.

If you do decide to close your farm, you can prolong the closing through a series of "Going Out of Business Sale-brations!" In fact, some furniture businesses have found these to be such successful events that they base their entire revenue on them.

People need to know they can trust you and your business. Therefore, jam-pack your advertisements with *wow*. Flashy and interactive media will draw in and seal the fate of new customers, as will discussion forums and brochures. If you cannot make any other improvements to your farm, plan to annually up the awesomeness-factor in your advertisements by 150 percent.

TAKE IT WITH YOU!

1. In your second year, you have the opportunity to be even more fantastic! So don't blow it.

2. Find ways to improve your farm in ways that fit your style: education, appearance, events, etc. The unicorns will appreciate the exciting shakeup, as long as they get to maintain their routines.

3. Going out of business is a last resort, but it can still be done with pizzazz.

4. Make your community presence full of zing!

READER'S NOTES:

_____

_____

_____

_____

_____

_____

_____

_____

_____

_____

_____

_____

CHAPTER 12

UNICORN EXPANSION

> *"The courage to follow your dream to completion is half the adventure. The other half is making sure your unicorns arrive with you."*
>
> —FARMER HARRY McCREADY,
> *THE UNICORN INCORPORATION MANIFESTO*, 1947

The preceding quote came from Farmer McCready, a pioneer in "unicorn-poration." Throughout his fifty-year career, he had endured business setbacks and unicorn strikes, yet he remained bound and determined to complete his adventure. And he did, passing away in 1952 from lung inflammation caused by sustained sparkle ingestion. At his death, his beloved unicorns stood around his bedside, and his million-dollar corporation flew their unicorn-emblazoned flags at half-mast to mourn the passing of their founder, visionary, and director of farming practices.

Inspired? You'd better be. And if you've made it this far in your dream, unicorns in tow, you have proven yourself worthy to take on the next exciting journey: expanding your enterprise.

EXPANSION OF YOUR UNICORN FARM

Farmer McCready expanded his farm operations by employing the unicorns in manual labor, building roads, buildings, and radio towers. He also knew how to grow his business based on changing times. For example, in the 1940s, his unicorns began assisting U.S. women in their jobs to support the military.

The reason this type of expansion worked so well is that it stayed true to its basic function: making tangible things with cheap labor and a certain degree of magic.

McCready had learned early on that his company could not do *all* things well, when he decided to introduce wine-making into his portfolio of industries in the 1920s. Even though the grapes that were stomped by the unicorns produced a higher quality wine than any other available, his business model did not translate for successful branding and distribution (FIG. 12.a.). Plus, Prohibition was still in full effect, so there was that.

FIGURE 12.a. *A unicorn stomping grapes to create amazing but unsuccessful sparkling wine.*

When it comes time for you to expand your farm, consider two options: Expand in the direction in which you are already going, or diversify your businesses. The first option is popular among those who want to stick with what they know, as well as those who are scared excrementless about any kind of change. The second option is for the savvy, the pioneers, and the pirates.

Neither option is better, of course, but the second option is much more glamorous. Just ask Farmer McCready and his long string of supermodel wives.

Option 1: For the Careful and Timid

Growing your business means spending more. The chart below demonstrates this phenomenon.

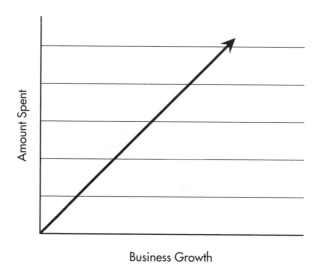

Business Growth

Therefore, plan to scale your operations. For example, if you are currently buying one ton of feed each year, and you are expanding into three farms, plan to buy three tons of feed each year.

One easy way to expand your farm without an initial investment is through unicorn reproduction. Sure, you will need to pay to raise the new acorns, but getting them into the world is much cheaper than buying a herd from a potentially unscrupulous unicorn dealer. So lower the lights in the stalls and let nature take its course. Depending on the breeds in those stalls, you will have enough new livestock somewhere in the next three years to create the services and products, or to simply be sold off to accommodate your expansion efforts.

To be truly successful, you may want to hire a mathematician to help you keep track of all the new numbers. Even better, you should hire a mathemagician. They cost about the same, and it is much more entertaining to watch the latter solve problems.

Your unicorns may be confused as they see you around less and less, and they will sense that something big is happening. Therefore, plan to invite them to all the grand openings so they can feel that they participated in this change *and* have a great time with the streamers, balloons, and bright colors.

Option 2: For the Daring, Fearless, and Attractive

This route will take you right into the heart of danger. You will explore territory charted only by a few hundred other people throughout all of unicorn-farming history, and you will walk away a wiser and, perhaps, extremely wealthier business owner. If you *can* walk away.

Yes, this is the life for a real unicorn farmer. And it is not for the fainthearted.

To begin identifying the direction in which to take your farm, consider all the businesses you would enjoy venturing into (FIG. 12.b.).

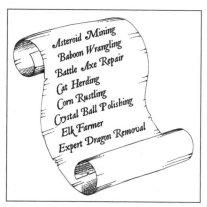

FIGURE 12.b. *A scroll of possible businesses.*

You can be either impulsive or strategic in your next step. Don't worry—both are extremely appealing to the opposite sex.

If you want to be impulsive, throw caution to the wind and open one of the businesses on your list. Have a grand opening.

If you want to be strategic, figure out your core values, then select from your list the businesses that fit with those core values. Consult with your mathemagician about your resources, then open one about which you feel most passionate. Have a grand opening.

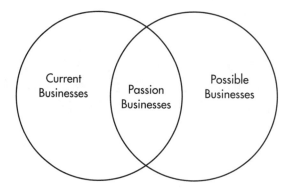

✒ *TESTIMONIAL* ✒
FARMER MCGLITTER GRABS LIFE BY THE HORN

After a freak trash-compactor accident where he lost his pinky toe at its knuckle, Mr. McGlitter declared, "I will never again miss a moment to live each day to the fullest!" So when he bought his first of many unicorn farms, he went all out with expanding it into all kinds of new territories. As a result, he was the first human to send a unicorn into deep sea, as well as the first researcher to discover that unicorns do not get the bends on the way back up. By year three of operations, his farm won the coveted "Most Enchanting Business Ventures" award from the Unicornomics Council—an honor typically bestowed on farms established for ten years or more.

Trying something new makes many a unicorn farmer feel alive. However, it has an adverse effect on the unicorns, who are inclined toward routine and familiarity. Make sure to buy them some extra toys or shiny things during this time to distract them from their complaining.

FRANCHISING

When unicorn farmers first think about expanding their businesses, many tremble at the thought of having to be in control. On the other end of the spectrum are the ones who crave ultimate control and refer to their business as their "empire." For the latter farmers, franchising may not be a fulfilling option. For everyone else, continue reading this section.

Franchising allows one central business to be copied by others for a fee. Plus, no owners can besmirch your name without you being able to rip ownership from their hands with your own iron fist. So perhaps the power-hungry unicorn emperors *could* enjoy this option.

If you decide to franchise, know who you are so you can know what your clones should look like. If someone comes to you and says, "I really like how you create unicorn-down pillows, and I'd like to become a franchise of your business where I do not make pillows but instead sell homemade muffins and peanut brittle," you know immediately whether or not this fits into your business model and values. (Hint: It probably does not.)

As time goes on, if you continue to accumulate those lucrative franchising fees, you may not have to wait until age eighty-seven to retire like the majority of unicorn farmers. In addition, if they are the right franchisees for your franchise, they will be helping your reputation and selling more of your goods and services. A hat trick of wins!

Meanwhile, have your mathemagician make sure that the correct amount of money is streaming in, and ask him from time to time to divide by zero. It's amazing what happens when he performs that trick!

UNICORNOMICS PRINCIPLE

Your Gross Farm Profit doesn't only include the work you do—it also includes the work other people do for you so you don't have to do work!

✑ CASE STUDY ✑

AL'S FRANCHISING FAILURE

Albert Ivan Korn had the perfect name for a unicorn horn—accessories-shop start-up: Al I. Korn's Alicorns. With such a great business name, Al tried to franchise his operations, but he had no plan or lawyer. He found the process of franchising so upsetting that he bailed after only one verbal agreement. That franchise continued to operate, though, and it patented all of the ideas Al had initially provided to it. By the time he realized what had taken place, there was no business left to franchise, as the franchise had already franchised operations from its own headquarters. Al learned to never again engage in verbal contracts, and he developed a phobia of unicorns.

TAKE IT WITH YOU!

1. To keep your unicorn businesses successful, stay true to their common core—your uni-core values.
2. If you aren't a risk-taker, your business can still be profitable. It will just be lacking in the "legacy" category.
3. If you are a risk-taker, don't stop without making history.
4. Franchising is magical: It creates money even when you aren't working.

READER'S NOTES:

_____

_____

_____

_____

_____

_____

_____

_____

_____

_____

_____

_____

_____

∽ PART 4 ∾
IN CONCLUSION

Evaluation is important, but it takes a lot of time and mental energy. If you do a good job the first time around, then you can save your time for celebrating that you rocked those goals.

If you don't do a good job the first time around, plan for some late nights of number crunching and investor-convincing. That should be punishment/incentive enough to do well the first time.

If you insist on ramping up to become the most successful unicorn farm enterprise in the history of both men *and* unicorns, then get those tables and graphs ready for some fantastic grand openings! Because that really is the magical key to success in the unicorn-farming industry.

Welcome aboard, unicorn farmer. May your colorful, mystical dreams come true as you turn them into a fiscally rewarding reality!

AFTERWORD

It has been an enchanted ride, hasn't it?

You have ridden the rainbow from unicorn-farmer wannabe to unicorn-farmer about-to-be. Your sparkling toolbelt is full of potential, and your lunchbox is packed with dreams. So, off to work you go, right?

Perhaps not.

Perhaps you have finished reading this manual and found yourself asking, "Am I truly ready for this life-transforming career?"

Perhaps you have identified more with the case studies of failed unicorn farmers than the testimonials of those who were successful.

Perhaps you have looked at your name and decided it isn't befitting of a unicorn farmer.

Perhaps you have not been able to hold any kind of a job for longer than five days, and the thought of living beings depending upon you for sustenance is triggering a minor coronary event.

These are valid concerns, and you aren't alone in your fears. In a recent study, 37 percent of unicorn farmers confessed to an emergency hospital visit the night before their first farm-related purchase. Nevertheless, no unicorn-megalopoly mogul has ever dominated a nation's economy without risking that first scary step.

Or maybe you have finished reading this manual and simply cannot wait to get started. You are skimming this Afterword to see if there are any final tips for financial super-prosperity, poised to race out the door in pursuit of a roving band of investors who will put monetary wheels on your aspirations. If this is you, here is that final tip: To boost both productivity and morale, invest in cloud-infused shoes for your unicorns.

Lastly, maybe you just aren't sure. You aren't afraid, but you aren't exactly excited by the idea of venturing into the unicorn business. If this is you and you also answered mostly d's in the "Which Type of Unicorn Farmer Are You?" quiz, do the entire unicorn farming industry a favor and select a different vocation. Elk farming is always an option.

Raising unicorns is a fascinating, obscenely high-paying adventure, but not everyone is invited. Only those who are willing to grab life by the horn and gallop past the mediocre into a world of unlimited possibility shall hear and respond to the entrepreneurial call of the unicorn.

Are you ready to embrace the awesomeness?

UNICORN
FARMER'S
CALENDAR PAGES

JANUARY

1 New Year's Eve party cleanup	**2** Quarterly budget meeting	**3**	**4**	**5**	**6**	**7**
8	**9**	**10**	**11**	**12**	**13**	**14**
15 Stable cleaning	**16**	**17** Alicorn polishing	**18** Karmics: Floss teeth and alicorn	**19** Twinkletoes: De-glitter to remove sparkle buildup in ear canals	**20** Purebreds: Replen-ish butterfly dip's sugar water to attract but-terflies to flutter around tail and ears	**21** Gigglerumps: Beauty treatment/ Makeover
22	**23**	**24**	**25**	**26** Release new employee handbook, including human resources and unicorn resources policies	**27**	**28**
29	**30**	**31**				

FEBRUARY

		1		2 Groundhog Day: Visit Punxsutawney, PA, to support the cause of animals predicting the future	3	4
5 International Unicorn Show: Attend for announcement of latest models	**6**	**7**	**8**	**9**	**10** Acorn Day: Celebrate the birth of all acorns born within the past year	**11**
12	**13**	**14** Valentine's Day: Provide backup for Cupid	**15**	**16**	**17** Plant and fertilize flowers in open meadow	**18** New Unicorn Training: *Prancing for Beginners*
19	**20**	**21**	**22** Playdate with neighboring unicorn farm	**23**	**24** Free Wish Day for all visiting children under five years old	**25**
26	**27**	**28**	**29** Leap-Day party			

MARCH

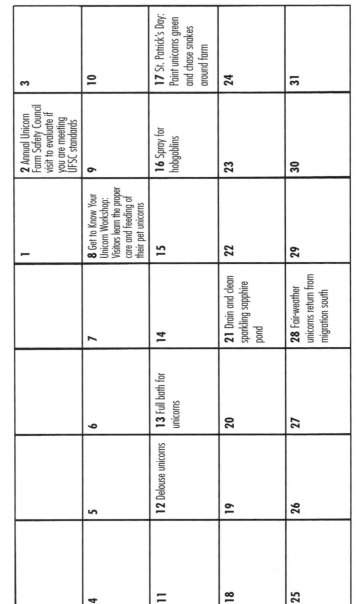

				1	2 Annual Unicorn Farm Safety Council visit to evaluate if you are meeting UFSC standards	3
4	5	6	7	8 Get to Know Your Unicorn Workshop: Visitors learn the proper care and feeding of their pet unicorns	9	10
11	12 Delouse unicorns	13 Full bath for unicorns	14	15	16 Spray for hobgoblins	17 St. Patrick's Day: Paint unicorns green and chase snakes around farm
18	19	20	21 Drain and clean sparkling sapphire pond	22	23	24
25	26	27	28 Fair-weather unicorns return from migration south	29	30	31

APRIL

1 Quarterly budget meeting	**2**	**3** Barn-raising day	**4**	**5** Annual checkups from unicorn vet	**6** Inoculations for unicorn farm staff: Vaccinate against measles, tetanus, and apathy	**7**
8	**9**	**10**	**11**	**12**	**13** Scavenger Hunt!	**14**
15 Taxes due (for U.S. farms)	**16**	**17**	**18**	**19**	**20**	**21**
22 Soften emerald green grass	**23**	**24**	**25**	**26**	**27**	**28** Unicorn Training: *How to Appear in Humans' Dreams without Seeming Out of Place*
29	**30**					

MAY

		1	2	3	**4** Test magic output: Compare against previous year's output figures	5
	7	**8**	**9** Shine double rainbow	**10** Annual customer-satisfaction survey	**11**	**12**
	14	**15**	**16**	**17**	**18**	**19**
6 Free gift with every purchase in unicorn farm gift shop						
13 Annual customer-satisfaction survey						
20	**21** Toy sort: Clean or toss all unicorn equipment	**22** Playdate with neighboring unicorn farm	**23**	**24**	**25**	**26**
27 Ice cream social	**28**	**29**	**30**	**31** Begin summer holiday season		

JUNE

					1 Finalize content for annual report	2
3	4	5		6 Half-Price Ride Day: Visitors ride one Twinkletoe or Purebred unicorn for 50 percent off the regular price	7	8	9
10	11	12		13 Full bath for unicorns	14	15 Publish annual report	16
17 Renew unicorn farm operating license	18	19		20	21 Golden hay rides	22	23
24	25	26		27	28 Unicorn Training: *We Aren't Horses: Avoiding Complicated Romances*	29 Release strategic plan for new fiscal year	30

1 Send annual report to investors, illustrated executive summary to unicorn enthusiasts	**2** Quarterly budget meeting	**3**	**4**	**5**	**6**	**7**
8	**9**	**10**	**11**	**12** Visit another unicorn farm: Explore potential for trades and purchases	**13**	**14**
15	**16**	**17**	**18** Karmics: Floss teeth and alicorn	**19** Twinkletoes: De-glitter to remove sparkle buildup in ear canals	**20** Purebreds: Replenish butterfly dip's sugar water to attract butterflies to flutter around tail and ears	**21** Gigglerumps: Beauty treatment / Makeover
22 Mating Week: Dim the stable lights to aid in breeding	**23**	**24**	**25**	**26**	**27**	**28**
29	**30**	**31**				

AUGUST

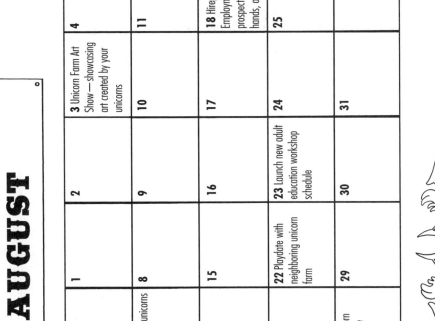

			1	2	3 Unicorn Farm Art Show — showcasing art created by your unicorns	4
5	6 Hoof cleanings followed by manicures and pedicures	7 Re-shoeing unicorns	8	9	10	11
12 Cupcake baking class	13	14	15	16	17	18 Hirepalooza: Employment fair for prospective groomers, hands, and trainers
19	20	21	22 Playdate with neighboring unicorn farm	23 Launch new adult education workshop schedule	24	25
26	27	28 New Unicorn Training: *Virgin Detection 101*	29	30	31	

SEPTEMBER

						1
2	3	4	5	6	7	8 Launch ad campaign to attract the last of the summer tourists
9	10 Making Crafts with Unicorns: Examples include dandelion chains, toothpick alicorns, and gumdrop houses	11	12	13 Full bath for unicorns	14	15 Meet with investors
16	17	18	19	20	21 Open adoption day at unicorn shelter	22
23	24	25	26 Research lab presentation on latest findings and creations	27	28	29 End summer holiday season
30 Fair-weather unicorns migrate south						

OCTOBER

	1 Quarterly budget meeting	**2**	**3**	**4** Teambuilding retreat	**5**
26					
7	**8** Harvest golden hay for hayrides and rainbow hay for light snacks	**9** Harvest grapes for sparkling wine	**10**	**11** Photograph unicorns and unicorn farm staff for holiday card	**12**
13					
14	**15** Unicorn Training: *Don't Outrun the Rainbow: Learning to Slow Down in Life*	**16**	**17**	**18** Shave alicorns for health products	**19**
20					
21 Family Fun Fest with UniCorn Maze and Face Glittering	**22**	**23**	**24**	**25**	**26**
27					
28	**29**	**30**	**31**		

NOVEMBER

			1	2	3
4	**5** Launch campaign for unicorns to pull Santa's sleigh	**6** Begin training regimen in event Santa chooses unicorns over reindeer	7	8	9	10
11 Sparkleize wine and bottle it for holiday sales	12	13	**14** Renew advertising contracts with local media outlets	15	16	17
18 Cuddle Week: Seven days of affection and snuggling in the stables	19	20	21	22	23	24
25	**26** Follow up with Santa to emphasize commitment to cause	**27**	**28** Playdate with neighboring unicorn farm	**29**	**30** Send out holiday cards	

DECEMBER

						1 Unicorn-drawn carriage rides (every day of the month)
2	3	4	5	6	7	8
9	10 Nonprofit outreach	11	12 Confirm schedule with Santa for sleigh pull	13 Full bath for unicorns	14	15
17	17	18	19	20 Unicorn Training: *Increasing the Accuracy of Your Wish Fulfillment*	21	22
23	24 If chosen, arrive at North Pole to begin delivering presents	25 If not chosen, send concession basket to reindeer with message, "We'll be back next year!"	26 Send surprise gifts to the kids whose parents gave them unsightly sweaters	27	28	29
30	31 New Year's Eve soiree					

RESOURCES

....

ORGANIZATIONS

Council of Unicornologists: An organization founded in 1747 devoted to the perpetuation of unicornological ethics, ideals, and data tracking

The Narwhal/Unicorn Peacekeeping Commission: International team appointed by the United Nations to maintain positive relations between the oft-battling mammals

Unicornomics: Research and development firm and unicorn farm dedicated to the art and science of successful raising and marketing of unicorns

Unicorn Show Association (USA): Regulator of parking and some concession stands at unicorn shows throughout the world

Unicorn Whisperers United (UWU): Professional organization and referral service of unicorn whisperers

SHOPPING

Sellers of Philip Seymour Hoffman Repellant: Obscure Novelty Outlet (Hong Kong), Baza's Bizarre Bazaar (Boulder, CO)

Sellers of Ye Olde-Fashioned Deluxe Farm Tool Kit: Marc & Mark's Fancy Unicorn Shoppe (Baltimore, MD), All the King's Unicorns (London, UK)

Sellers of Ye Olde-Fashioned Farm Tool Kit: Kay's Unicorncophony (Athens, GA), Farm, Field, & Fantasy (Winnepeg, MB)

BIBLIOGRAPHY

Farmer McGlitter's Guide to Spin-Doctoring Unicorn Scandals: A Public Relations Manual by Farmer McGlitter

From A(licorn) to U(nicorn): The New Owner's Guide to Everything Unicorn! by Farmer Colleen McKendrick

Statistics Don't Suck That Much—Really! by Mathemagician Maurice Magnifico

Unicorn Farming for Novices by Farmer Stephanie McMahon

The Unicorn Incorporation Manifesto by Farmer Harry McCready

GLOSSARY

Acorn: Unicorn baby, which is naturally born without an alicorn

Alicorn: The horn of a unicorn

Assembly of the Unicorn Keepers: The higher council to which all unicorns report, available to arbitrate cases, deliver decrees, and plan belated birthday surprise parties

El Chupacabra: A sneaky blood-drinking creature and one of the two known enemies of unicorns (translated from Spanish as "goat-sucker")

ESAH: The four-step process to preventing a unicorn uprising: Eye contact, Slow approach, Arms extended, Hug

Gigglerump: One of the four breeds of unicorn, possessing a stout body, asymmetrical face, one short horn over the right eye, unkempt mane, and clumsy disposition

Karmic: One of four breeds of unicorn, possessing an ivory body, red eyes, one horn that divides in two at the tip, and irritable disposition

Mathemagician: A mathematician who does illusions, making your bookkeeping and data-tracking always entertaining

Omnicorn, The: The supreme ruler over all unicorns and the Assembly of the Unicorn Keepers

Pegacorn: A pegasus-unicorn hybrid

Philip Seymour Hoffman: Award-winning actor and one of the two known enemies of unicorns

Polycorn posse: A group of unicorns

Purebred: One of four breeds of unicorn, possessing a white body, blue or lavender eyes, a single horn upon its forehead, glitter in its mane, and a kind disposition

Red licorice: The only kind of licorice chewed by unicorn farmers

Trojan Unicorn: A robotic, life-sized, unicorn-shaped decoy that, once accepted into your competition's care, allows for inconspicuous and effective spying on their premises

Twinkletoe: One of four breeds of unicorn, possessing an entire essence of glitter, green eyes, a single horn upon its forehead, and a disposition toward entertaining

Unicorn Express: Mail delivery system using unicorns as transportation

Unicornomics: The study of raising and marketing unicorns (originating from the research and development firm and unicorn farm by the same name)

Unicorn pie: Pie chart used to display statistics on your unicorn farm

Unicorn-poration: A term coined by Farmer Harry McCready to define unicorn-related businesses, especially those that involve unicorns in the business itself

Unicorn Richter Scale: A scale created by Charles Richter prior to his earthquake measurement to determine the total impact of a selected group of unicorns

Unmitigated novelty: The hyper-kitschy type of products and reputation unicorn farmers must avoid in their development, marketing, and distribution efforts

INDEX

....

AUTHOR'S
ACKNOWLEDGMENTS

I want to thank all the unicorns, unicorn farmers, and unicorn-farm employees who made this book such a success.

To my Purebreds: Mom and Dad, who never doubted that unicorns were, indeed, marketable. To Nana, who left this world before she could read this manual, but whose cheerful heart was enviable by even the most gleeful of unicorns.

To my Twinkletoes: Joe and Brian at The Motor Lodge in Prescott, who kept me sequestered and inspired; Amy Jean for the sacrificial loan of her Unicorn Princess.

To my Karmics: Tonia, who fiercely keeps the dream alive; Steve for being an awesome brother who taught me that everything—even beer bottles and alligators—is sentient.

To my Gigglerump: Kevin Hedgpeth, illustrator extraordinaire, whose artistic renderings truly capture life on a unicorn farm.

To the unicorn farmers who shared their vast wealth of knowledge: Stephanie H.nicorn, Barbara, Kerri, and the ever-wise expert, Farmer McGlitter.

To the unicorn-farm employees: Matt Glazer, my developmental editor and thought generator; Bob Pimm, the lawyer every unicorn farm needs.

To the Creator of all unicorns, the first and last word on—and epitome of—awesomeness.

And to my Director of Applications and co-conspirator, Bob. You bring more magic into my life than our entire chain of unicorn farms and brand of delicious unicorn-inspired preserves.

ILLUSTRATOR'S
ACKNOWLEDGMENTS

I'd like to thank those family members, friends, and aides who made my artistic blandishments for this book a successful endeavor.

To my wife, Gail, who provided the critiques, production assistance, and good-natured chiding required to help me accomplish this project.

To my sons, Jacob and Aaron, who selflessly allowed my illustration work to encroach on our playtime.

To Jessica S. Marquis, who believed that my graphic chicanery could be harnessed to create unique unicorn illustrations.

To Matt Glazer, who wrangled unicorn pictures and magical spreadsheets.

I'd also like to extend special thanks to those organizations that provided material aid in my research on unicorn anatomy:

To the Royal Toolingham Athenaeum, for providing me with a transcript of the mysterious Blatherstone manuscript on early unicornology.

To the Maguffin University Library, who loaned me a copy of E.S.S. Mistvale's monograph, *Fossil Horned Equines of the Upper Eocene Douglas-Homer Formation.*

DAILY BENDER

Want Some More?

Hit up our humor blog, The Daily Bender, to get your fill of all things funny—be it subversive, odd, offbeat, or just plain mean. The Bender editors are there to get you through the day and on your way to happy hour. Whether we're linking to the latest video that made us laugh or calling out (or bullshit on) whatever's happening, we've got what you need for a good laugh.

If you like our book, you'll love our blog. (And if you hated it, "man up" and tell us why.) Visit The Daily Bender for a shot of humor that'll serve you until the bartender can.

Sign up for our newsletter at

www.adamsmedia.com/blog/humor

and download our Top Ten Maxims No Man Should Live Without.